INTRODUCTION

Throughout thousands of years of human history, people have invented machines and devices that have changed and improved our everyday lives, or that have made jobs easier to do or quicker to complete.

Inventions range from the simple, such as the compass and the paper clip, to the very complex, such as the factory robot and the hospital body scanner. They are used in every possible place, from the depths of the oceans to space stations in orbit high above the Earth, and from the kitchen worktop to the hospital operating theatre.

People have also made discoveries about our world, such as metals hidden inside rocks, electricity, and invisible radio waves, all of which have made possible things such as iron tools, electric motors and mobile telephones.

Left: The light bulb revolutionalized everyday life. It gave people safe lighting at the flick of a switch. The light bulb has become a symbol for a new idea!

Below: The intricate cogs inside a watch are part of a time-keeping machine. The invention of clocks and watches was vital for organizing time as the world became industrialized.

Inventions and discoveries have completely transformed our world and the way we live. They allow us to live in inhospitable parts of the planet, to build giant structures such as skyscrapers and stadiums, to mass-produce millions of items every day, and to cure diseases and repair injuries.

The biggest transformation has come in communications, where machines have made the world seem a much smaller place to us than it seemed to our ancestors. A century ago most people had never left their own villages, towns or cities, and had only spoken to local people. They could send letters, but a message took months to reach the other side of the world. Now we can actually travel to the other side of the world in less than a day, and we can phone or e-mail to anywhere in the world in an instant.

To a person who lived a hundred years ago, the machines we use today would seem incredible. It is hard to predict how new inventions will change the world in the future, but we can be sure that in another hundred years there will be machines that would seem incredible to us today.

Above: The invention of the silicon chip in the 1950s allowed millions of microscopic electronic components to be fitted on a tiny wafer of silicon.

Left: The invention of the computer was as important as the invention of the wheel. Today, commerce, industry, communications and scientific research could not function without computers.

Above: Aircraft are among the most complex machines that we have built. A Boeing 747 contains millions of parts made from hundreds of different materials.

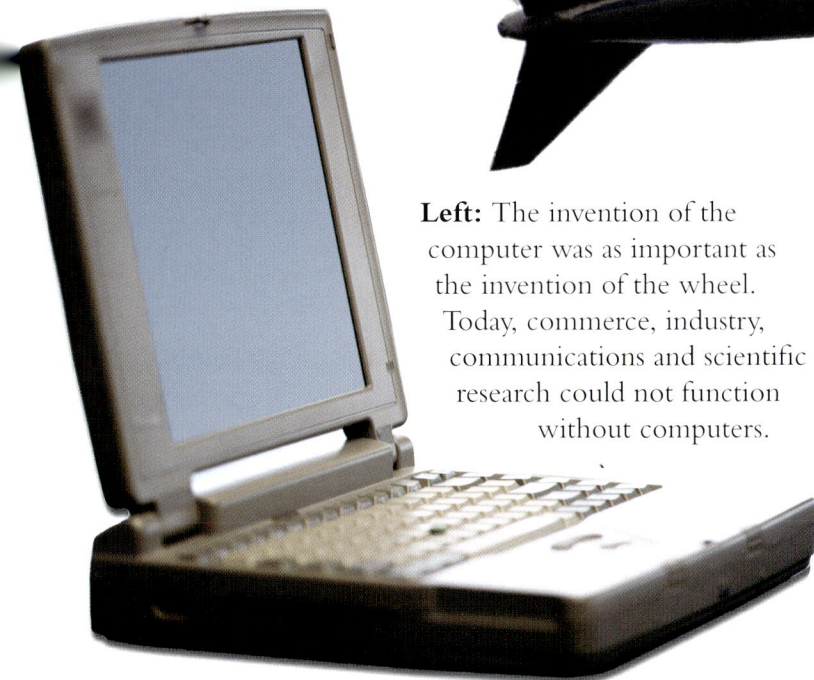

INVENTIONS & DISCOVERIES

SHAPING OUR WORLD

MANY things you do, from reading this book to flying abroad on holiday, would be impossible without the work of inventors. Without Johannes Gutenberg who, in the mid-1400s, invented the first printing press in Europe, this book could not have been printed. In 1903, the brothers Orville and Wilbur Wright were the first people to build and fly an aeroplane successfully. The aeroplane that takes you on holiday could not have been built without their pioneering work.

Human beings have been inventing things for thousands of years. The wooden wheel was first used as a means of transport 5,500 years ago. Inventors have also improved upon existing inventions, to shape the world we live in today. Nowadays trains and cars travel on wheels made of metal and rubber at speeds of up to about 200kph. This chapter is about how inventions have formed today's world.

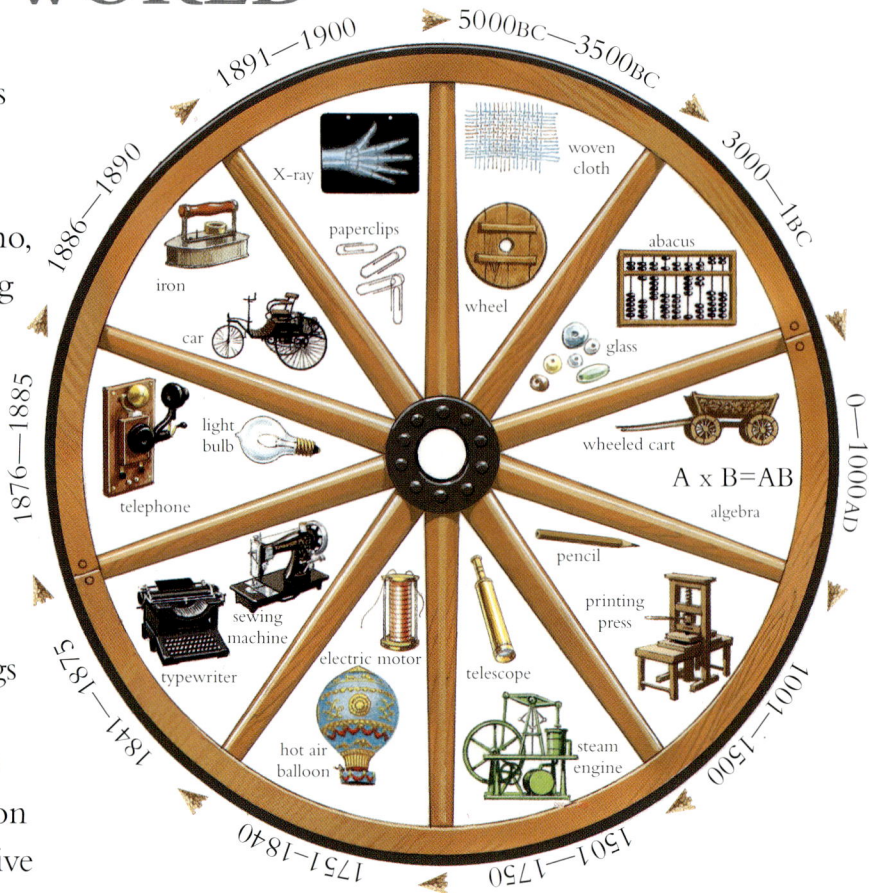

Wheel labels, clockwise from top:
5000BC—3500BC • 3000—1BC • 0—1000AD • 1001—1500 • 1501—1750 • 1751—1840 • 1841—1875 • 1876—1885 • 1886—1890 • 1891—1900

woven cloth • abacus • glass • wheeled cart • A x B=AB algebra • pencil • printing press • telescope • steam engine • hot air balloon • electric motor • sewing machine • typewriter • telephone • light bulb • car • iron • paperclips • wheel • X-ray

Moving on

In this wheel are some of the objects invented from 4000BC to AD1900 that have fundamentally changed our lives. Follow the arrowheads to see the progression of invention through the ages.

Clean and dry

In the past, people washed clothes by putting them in a tub of hot water and rubbing them with soap. William Sillars invented the first machine for washing clothes in 1890. By turning the big wheel on the lid of the tub, a person could turn the long pegs on the underside of the lid. The moving pegs swirled the clothes around in the tub and so washed out the dirt. The first electric washing machine that washes and spins in a tub, was invented in 1901 by Alva J. Fisher.

modern washing machine

1890 washing machine

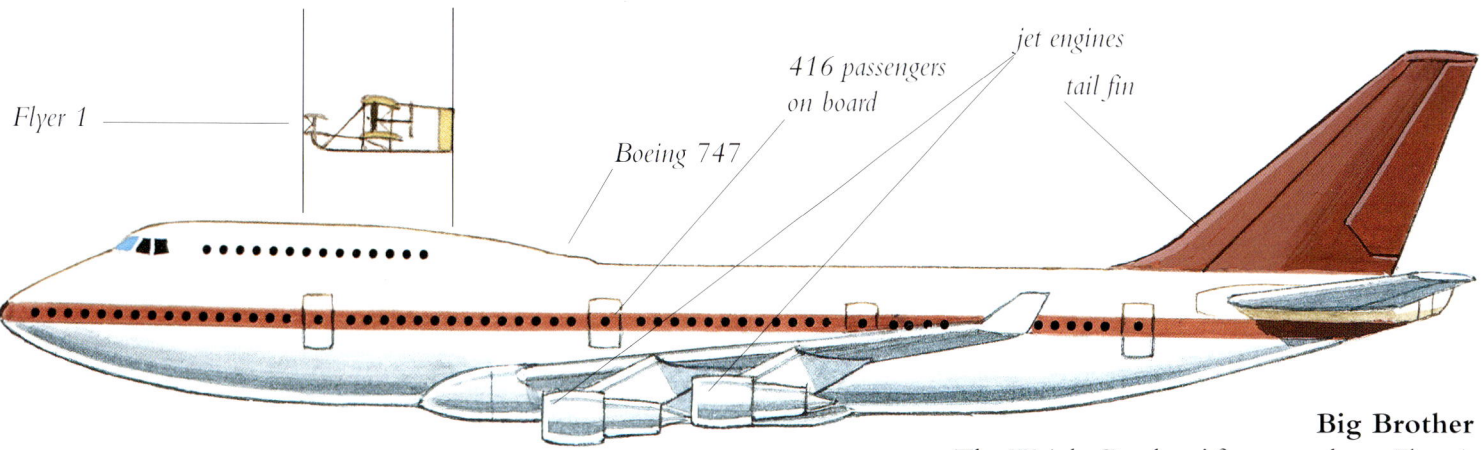

Flyer 1

Boeing 747

416 passengers on board

jet engines

tail fin

Big Brother

The Wright Brothers' first aeroplane, *Flyer 1*, was only 6.4m long. A modern *Boeing 747* is over 10 times bigger, and is almost 71m long. Only one person could fly on *Flyer 1*, while a *Boeing 747-400* can carry 416 passengers. Most modern passenger aircraft, such as the *Boeing*, are powered by jet engines. The jet engine was invented by Sir Frank Whittle in 1930.

It's good to talk

People can make telephone calls from wherever they want using a modern cellular phone such as the one seen here (*right*). The first telephone was invented by Alexander Graham Bell in 1876. He is seen in this engraving. He is testing the first telephone line to run between New York and Chicago, United States, in 1892. Bell's telephone sent voice messages along wires. To make a call, the user's phone had to be connected to a telephone wire. Cellular phones use radio waves and do not need wires.

MAKING LIFE EASIER

WITHOUT the development of bricks and mortar, it would not be possible to build the houses we live in today. People in modern houses, schools, offices and factories can turn on lights and heaters at the flick of a switch, turn taps for water, and look out through windows. In the 1700s and before, people had to fetch water from wells. Today water comes into buildings in pipes under the ground. Before there were electric lights, people used to light candles or lamps burning olive or whale oil.

The wires and pipes that supply electricity, water and gas to buildings today were invented in the 1800s. Many different people took part in their invention. The first electric power station was built in New York in 1884, based on the ideas of Thomas Edison. In the early 1800s, William Murdock, a British inventor, was the first person to set up a factory that produced gas for lighting streets and buildings. In the 1800s too, many people in cities were affected by diseases, such as cholera, that were caused by poor hygiene. Sewer pipes were built to carry drain water away from cities to treatment plants.

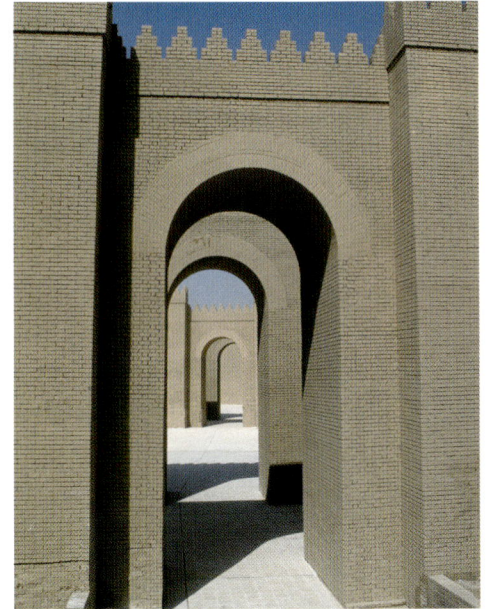

Straight and narrow
People used bricks to build gateways such as this 5,000 years ago in the part of the Middle East now called Iraq. These bricks made strong walls that could stand for many years.

Built to last
Gates in the German city of Trier (Trèves) were built almost 2,000 years ago. The mortar (cement) that holds the stones in the gates together was invented by the Romans, who then ruled all of France and parts of Germany. The long-lasting strength of mortar is an important reason why so many ancient Roman buildings have survived to this day.

Onwards and upwards
People are lifting blocks of stone on a winch, standing on scaffolding and cutting stone at the top of the tower in this illustration from the 1400s. Winches and scaffolding made it easier to lift heavy weights and keep stone in place.

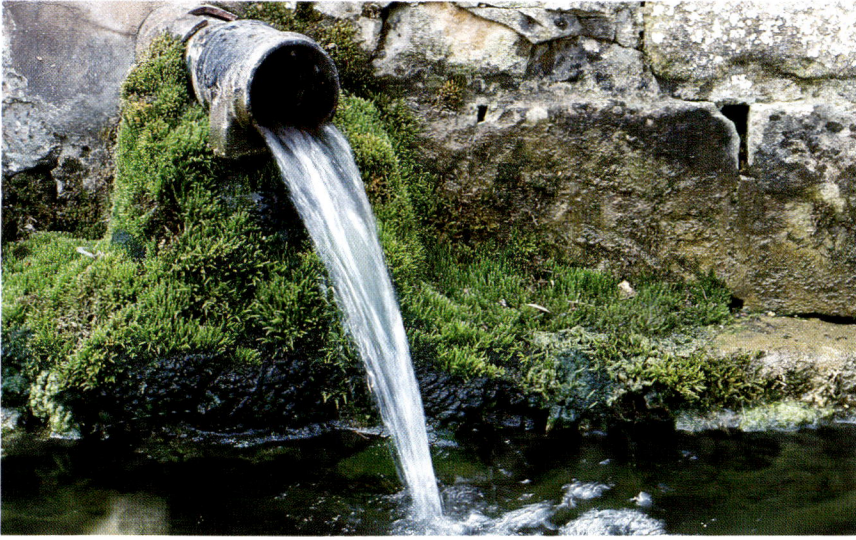

Dangerous metal

Lead was used for centuries to make the pipes through which water flowed from reservoirs to houses and public buildings such as baths. Lead dissolves in water and harms the health of the people who drink it. Since the 1950s, plastic water pipes have been used as a safer alternative.

Letting in light

Roman glass tiles, such as these, were made 2,000 years ago. Ways to make sheets of clear glass for windows were not found until the 1200s. In the 1800s, the British scientist, Michael Faraday, invented ways of making really large panes of glass.

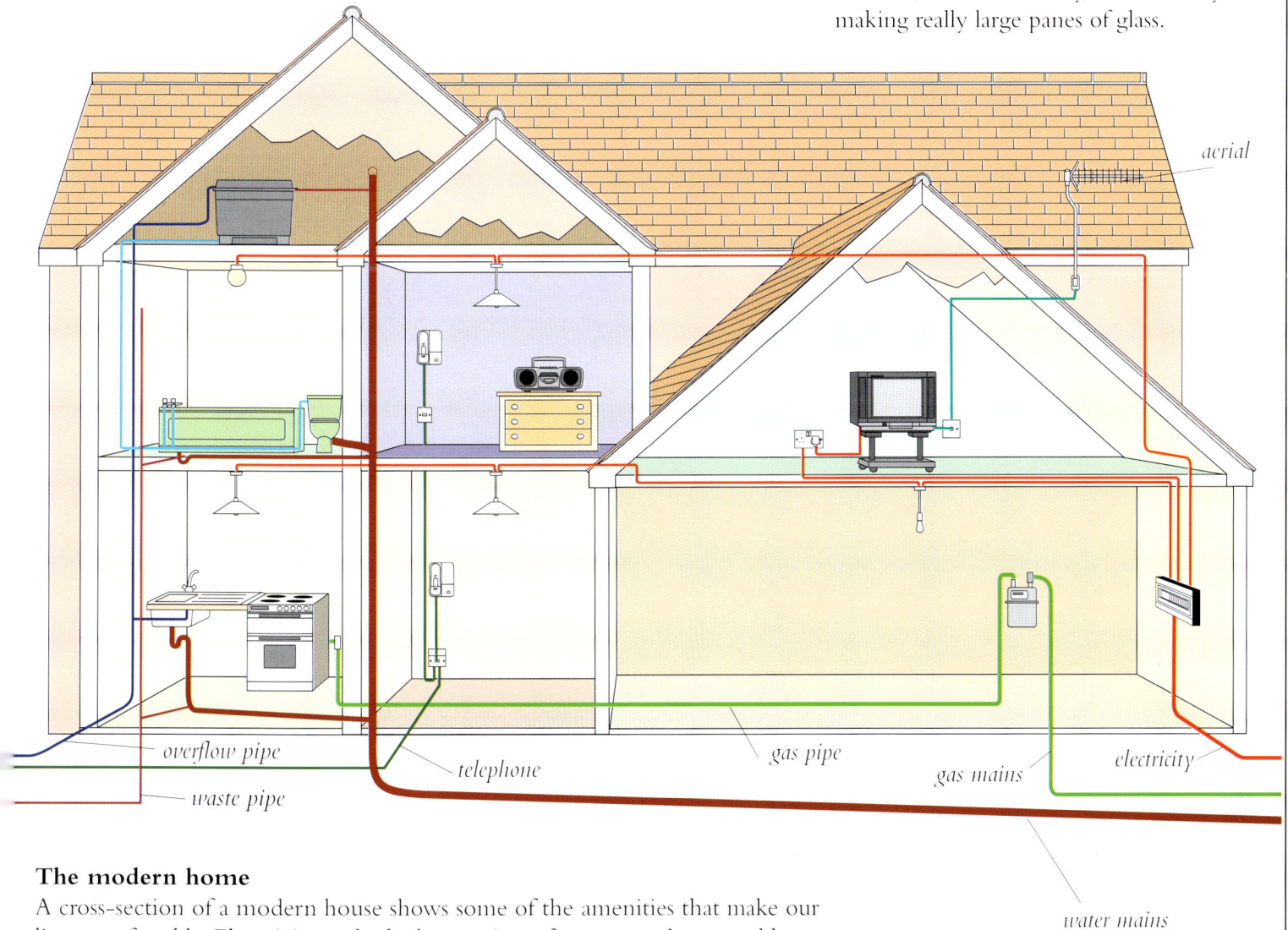

aerial

overflow pipe

telephone

gas pipe

electricity

gas mains

waste pipe

water mains

The modern home

A cross-section of a modern house shows some of the amenities that make our lives comfortable. Electricity and telephone wires often run underground but can be carried on poles and pylons from power stations.

BUILDING FOR STRENGTH

A PLATFORM bridge was one of the earliest human inventions, and was probably first used tens of thousands of years ago. People laid a tree trunk or a single slab of stone across narrow rivers or steep gullies to make travelling across easier. Many modern platform bridges are hollow and made of steel. The model here shows how thin folded sheets make a strong, hollow platform. If you stand on a simple platform bridge, the downward force of your weight makes it sag in the middle. Too much weight can snap a flat wooden plank or crack a stone slab.

Arch bridges, however, as the second project shows, are not flat and they do not sag when loaded. They curve up and over the gap that they span. The Romans were among the first to build arch bridges from many separate stone blocks more than 2,000 years ago. The shape of the bridge holds the stone blocks together. Pushing down on the centre of the bridge creates forces which push outwards so that the load is borne by the supports at either side.

A strong bridge
The Rainhill Bridge spanned the Liverpool and Manchester railway in 1832. It was made by fitting stone blocks around a wooden scaffold. The bridge could support itself when workers hammered the keystone at the very top into place.

MAKE A PLATFORM

You will need: scissors, stiff card, ruler, pen, 2 boards 20x20cm, modelling clay.

Your platform is stronger than a platform bridge because it is supported on four sides. Without this support it would sag in the middle.

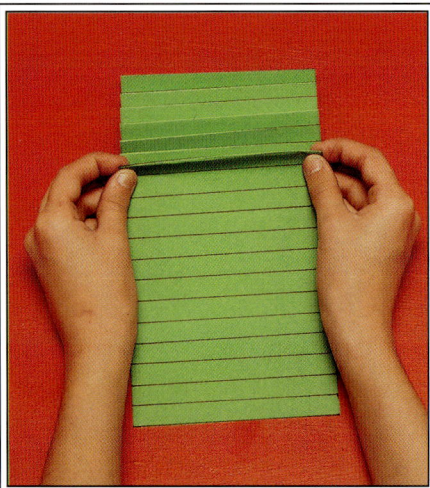

1 Cut out four strips of card 40x10cm. With a ruler and pen, draw lines 1cm apart across each card. Fold each card back and forth across the lines to form zigzag pleats.

2 Lay one board flat on the table. Stand a piece of pleated card upright along the board's edges. Repeat for the other three sides. Use modelling clay to secure each corner.

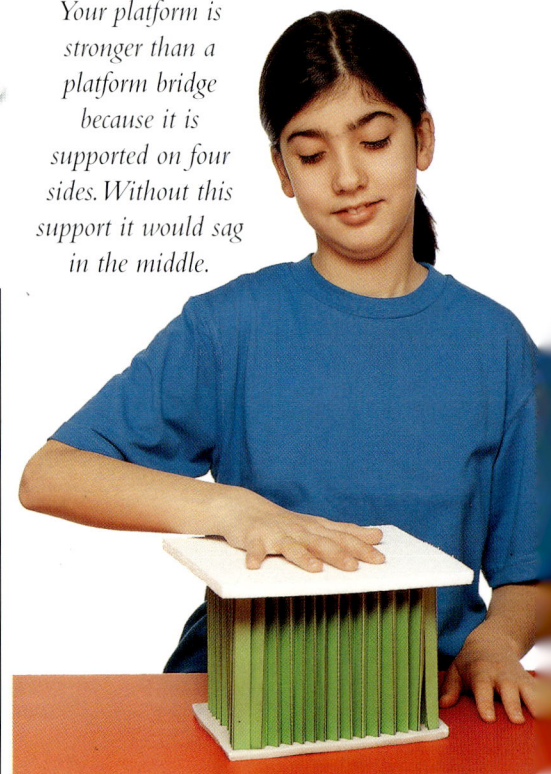

3 When all sides of the platform are in place, lay the second board on top. Push downwards with your hand. Pleating the card has made the platform very strong.

MAKE AN ARCH

You will need: 2 house-bricks, ruler, sand, 6 wooden toy building blocks, builder's plaster, water, plastic spoon, plastic knife.

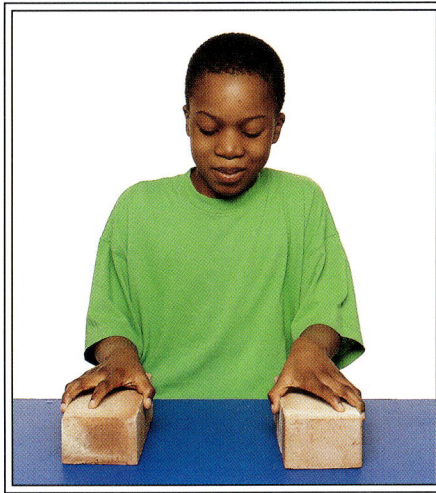

1 Although it is not shown in this picture, it would be a good idea to cover the table with newspaper first of all. Place the two bricks on the table. They should be about 20cm apart.

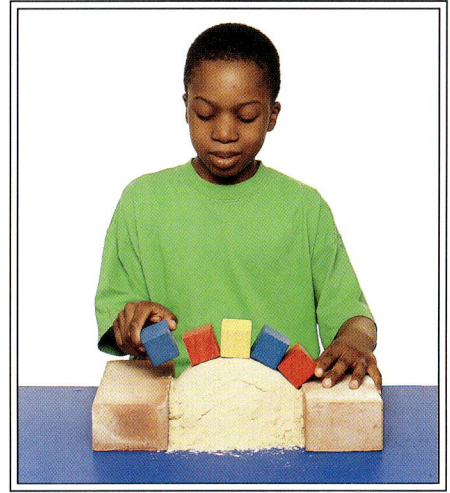

2 Pile up sand between the bricks and smooth it with your hands to make a curved mound. Place the wooden blocks side by side across the sand. The bricks should touch the outer blocks.

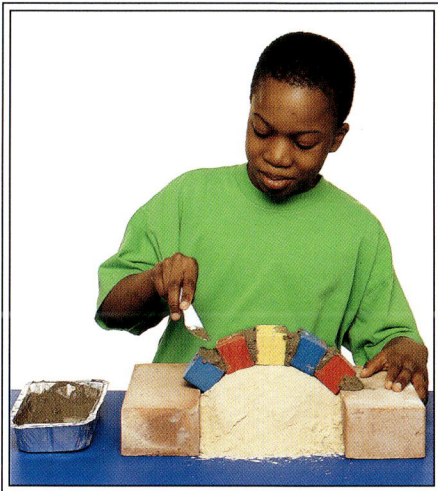

Like stone blocks in real bridges, the wooden toy blocks make a remarkably strong curve.

3 Notice that the inner blocks touch each other and have V-shaped gaps between them. Mix the plaster with water until it forms a stiff paste. Use the knife to fill the gaps between the blocks with paste.

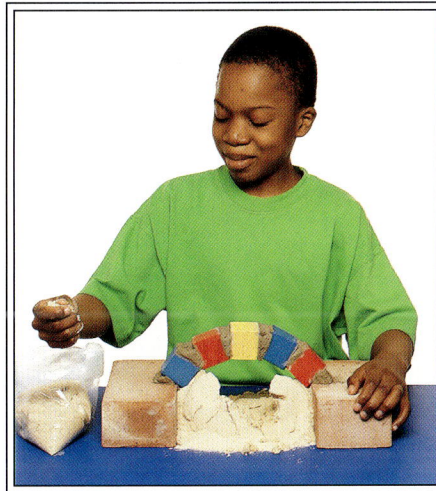

4 Make sure you have filled each space where the arch meets the bricks. Wait for the plaster to dry. Once dry, remove the sand from underneath the arch.

5 Push down on the arch and feel how firm it is. The weight that you are putting on the bridge is supported by the two bricks at the side. This bridge is stronger than the platform bridge and does not sag in the middle.

HOME IMPROVEMENTS

E ARLY humans lived in caves or shelters made from stones, wood or earth. They first discovered how to start a fire by rubbing sticks together. Fire provided them with warmth and a way to cook. The earliest houses with permanent walls, roofs and windows were built in villages such as Catal Hüyük in southern Turkey around 8,000 years ago. People there washed with hot water, had fireplaces in the middle of rooms and slept on shelves built against the walls of the houses.

Furniture, such as beds, chairs and tables, was first made by the ancient Egyptians. The ancient Romans built huge public baths and even had central heating 2,000 years ago. The basic design of homes has not changed very much since then. However, houses in Europe did not have chimneys until the 1200s and glass windows were unusual until the 1400s. It was not until the 1800s that many houses were built with indoor plumbing, and electric wiring was not built into the walls of houses until the 1900s.

Let there be light
This ancient Greek lamp is similar to those people used all over the world for thousands of years to light their homes. Lamps such as this burn olive oil. The flame they give is smoky and not very bright. Candles were also used for lighting in homes as early as 5000BC.

handle *cistern*

water flows down a pipe into the toilet

toilet

Finding the key
Homes need strong locks to keep valuables safe inside. The lock shown in this picture was invented by Joseph Bramah in 1787. It was the safest lock ever invented at the time. He boasted that he would give a reward to anyone who could pick the lock (unlock it without a key). It was 67 years before anyone succeeded.

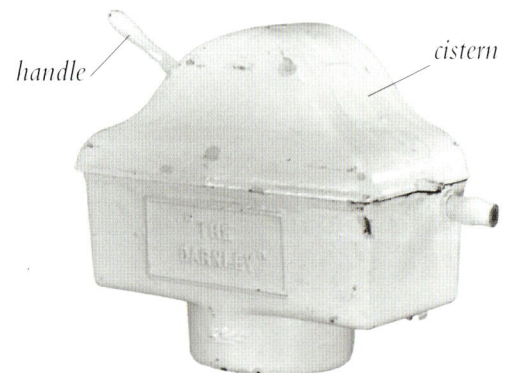

Flushed with success
The earliest toilets that are known about are more than 4,000 years old. They were found at Harappa and Mohenjo-Daro in Pakistan. Joseph Bramah, who invented the lock, invented the first flush toilet in 1778. This glazed ceramic (pottery) toilet was manufactured in 1850. It used water kept in a cistern (small water tank) above the toilet seat.

1993 vacuum cleaner

1910 vacuum cleaner

HOOVER

VORTEX

Crisp creases

For over 2,000 years, people have heated flattened pieces of iron to press on to clothes to smooth out wrinkles. In the past, people heated the iron on a fire or on a stove. In the late 1800s, inventors found a way to heat an iron using electricity. This electric iron was first produced in 1903.

Dust buster

Keeping homes clean has always been a concern. Prehistoric people threw their rubbish on to heaps at the edges of villages. In the 1900s, ways of using a vacuum (airless space) to suck in dirt were invented. This early vacuum cleaner, called the Daisy, was first made in 1910. It worked by using a bellows (pump for sucking out air). Modern vacuum cleaners, such as the 1993 Hoover, use power from an electric motor to suck dirt into a bag.

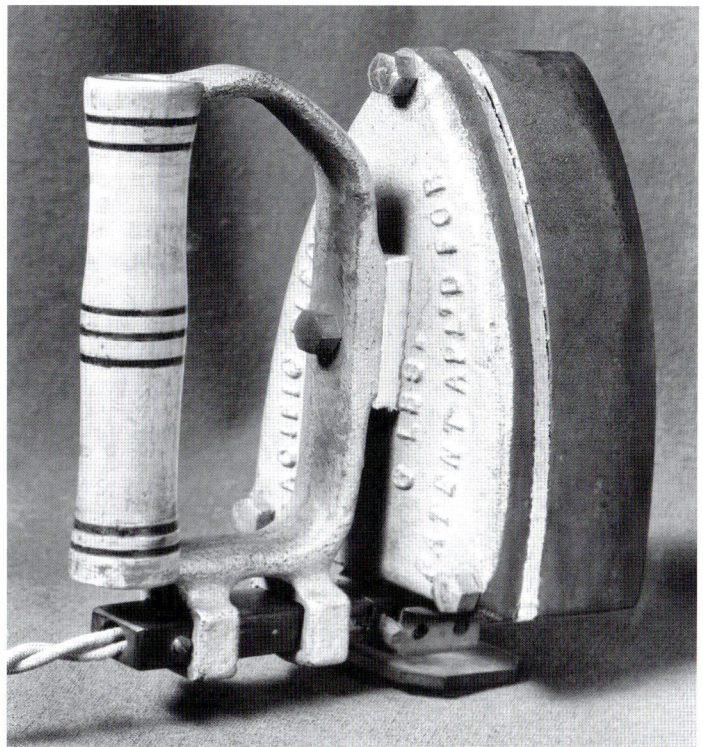

FACT BOX

• People living about 4,500 years ago in the cities of Harappa and Mohenjo-Daro in Pakistan had proper bathrooms in their public buildings. The well-planned cities were built with running water and drains under the streets.

• The oldest known type of lock, called a pin tumbler, is at least 4,000 years old. The oldest example was discovered in Nineveh, Iraq. Locks of this kind were used by the ancient Egyptians and are still used today in some parts of the world.

• Before people in cities had plumbing, they collected waste water in bowls and threw it out of the window into the street. Sometimes the muck fell on other people's heads.

WEAVING

Secret silk

For centuries, weaving silk was a secret known only to the people of China. They learned how to create fine, richly coloured cloth of the kind seen in this banner. It was buried 2,000 years ago.

Almost every kind of cloth is made by weaving. Threads made out of plant material such as cotton, or animal fleece such as wool, are woven on a loom. The oldest pieces of cloth known were found in Switzerland and are estimated to be about 7,000 years old. Before people invented ways to make cloth, they wore the skins of the animals they hunted, to keep warm and dry.

The cotton plant grew plentifully in Egypt and India 5,000 years ago. People there invented ways to weave it into clothing. In other parts of the world clothes were made from the wool of sheep or goats. The flax plant was also used to make cloth called linen. In China silk was woven as long as 4,500 years ago. In the 1700s, several inventions made it much easier to spin and weave both cotton and wool thread. These inventions allowed cloth to be made in much larger quantities than ever before. In the 1900s, artificial fibres such as nylon were invented that allowed new kinds of cloth to be made.

1300s spinning wheel

Fine thread

Silk is made from the thread that forms the cocoon (covering) spun around themselves by silk moth caterpillars. The cocoons are gathered and washed, and then the thread is unwound. The threads are plaited together to make strong thread for weaving. This Chinese painting from 500 years ago shows women spinning silk thread.

Spin me a yarn

The plant fibres or animal hair from which most cloth is made have to be spun together to make them strong. This is called yarn. In the 1300s, people in Europe first began to use spinning wheels such as this to spin thread. Experts believe wheels like this were first invented in India about 4,000 years ago.

1769 Arkwright spinning machine

Fast and furious

In the 1700s machines were invented that made it possible to weave cloth far more quickly than before. This meant that thread had to be spun more quickly. In 1769, Richard Arkwright invented a spinning machine that used horse power to turn pulleys and rollers. It spun thread much more quickly than on a spinning wheel.

Power weaving

A factory is fitted with some of the first large-scale weaving machines. Large weaving machines powered by steam engines were invented in the 1800s. These machines produced much more cloth than was possible using older ways of weaving. However, the people who looked after the machines in factories like this had to work very long hours in conditions that were often dangerous.

Stretch and bend

Clothes made from wool or plant fibres could be stiff and heavy to wear. Modern clothes made from synthetic fibres are designed to be more comfortable. The clothes this woman is wearing for exercising are made from Lycra, invented in 1953. It is very flexible and ideal to wear when you need to be able to bend.

Lycra

Smooth and shiny

This boy is wearing a raincoat made from polyvinyl chloride (PVC), a kind of plastic invented in 1913. New ways of making material were invented in the 1900s. New kinds of thread called synthetic (artificial) fibre were made from chemicals, not from plants and animal wool. The materials had names such as nylon and polyester.

CLEVER COOKS

PEOPLE cook food, especially meat, because it kills any germs, which makes it safer to eat. Until about 8,000 years ago the only way to cook meat was by roasting. People pushed a spit (metal rod) through an animal's body and held it over a fire while they turned the meat to cook it all over. The Chinese learned 3,000 years ago how to cook many different kinds of food using the Chinese *wok* (a metal cooking bowl). The ancient Egyptians knew how to bake bread in an oven 5,000 years ago. By the time of the ancient Greeks, people cooked using ovens, saucepans and frying pans. Not surprisingly, the first ever cookery book was written 2,300 years ago by the ancient Greek, Archestratus. Cooking methods changed very little for the next 2,000 years.

Ways of preserving food by freezing were invented in the 1800s and have changed the way people eat. Foods that had only been available in certain seasons could then be eaten all year round. Nowadays people can buy food cooked in advance and heat it up in a few minutes in a microwave oven.

Open-air eating
The Dutch artist Pieter Brueghel the Younger painted village people eating together in the 1500s. The huge cooking pot in the background of the painting was used to cook thick soups or stews over open fires.

Mass catering
In medieval Europe many people lived together in monasteries or castles. Cooking was done in huge kitchens such as this. Large fireplaces made it easier to feed many people quickly. These kitchens continued to be used up until the 1800s, as shown in this drawing of 1816.

Quick cuppa
Tea was first mixed with boiling water as a drink in China 2,000 years ago. It became popular in Europe in the 1600s and is now drunk all over the world. Boiling water in a kettle became much faster in the 1900s when electric kettles like this one were invented.

heat-proof handle

1921 electric kettle

spout

electric element

socket

Long-lasting soup

People have known ways of preserving food (keeping it edible over time) for thousands of years. Meat and fish were salted or dried. Fruit and vegetables were stored in the dark or cooked and then sealed in bottles. In the early 1800s, the Frenchman Nicolas Appert found a new way of keeping food fresh. He sealed it into steel cans, as the men in this factory in the mid–1800s are doing.

Frosty food

Freezing keeps food fresh for a long time. Ice cut out from huge blocks was used in Roman times to keep food fresh, but melted quickly. A number of inventors in the 1800s found ways of using air and liquids to flow round a box and keep it cold indefinitely. Electricity was used in the first refrigerator in 1934.

1934 refrigerator

Ready in a flash

Microwave ovens cook food faster than any ordinary cooker. Scientists invented this way of using radio waves to heat food in the 1940s. By the 1950s, the first microwave ovens were being sold.

Instant oven

Before the invention of gas cookers, ovens had to be fuelled with wood or coal each morning which meant a lot of hard work. In the 1800s inventors discovered how to make gas from coal and store it safely so that it could be fed through pipes to people's houses. Modern gas cookers like this one are linked up to gas pipes. The owner just turns a valve and gas flows into the cooker where it is lit to provide instant heat for cooking.

STAYING WELL

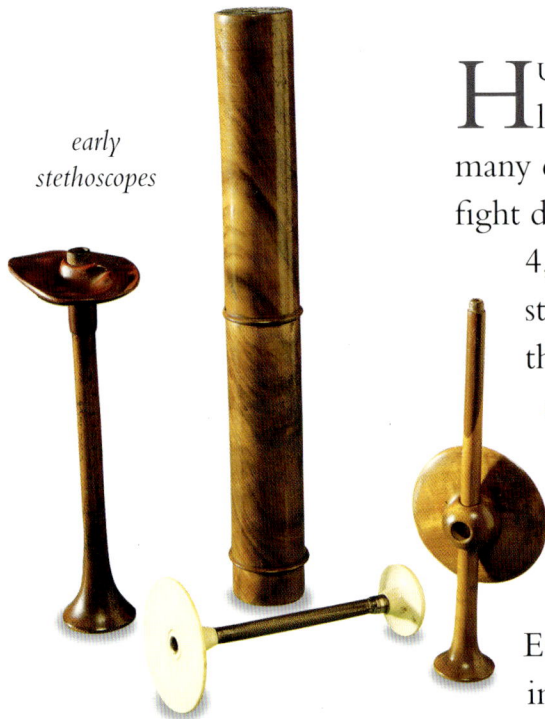

early stethoscopes

Human beings have been seeking new ways to cure illness and look after the sick for thousands of years. Today there are many drugs, machines and tools that doctors and nurses can use to fight disease. Yet in some ways little has changed. In ancient Egypt 4,500 years ago, a doctor would use compression (pressure) to stop someone bleeding. A modern doctor would do exactly the same thing. In China 2,000 years ago, doctors knew a great deal about the human body. They also practised a healing technique called acupuncture (inserting needles into parts of the body), which is still used all over the world.

By the 1500s Chinese doctors knew about some of the drugs that we use today. Medicine in the United States and Europe began to develop quickly in the 1800s. Ways were invented to stop germs infecting people and to anaesthetize (make unconscious) patients in surgery. In the 1920s, the British doctor Alexander Fleming discovered, by chance, the first antibiotics (drugs that kill germs). Many more antibiotics have been invented since then which treat different kinds of diseases.

Sounds under the skin

The French doctor René Laënnec invented a hollow tube in the early 1800s that allowed him to hear the sounds inside a patient's chest and heart. It was called a stethoscope. Four different kinds can be seen in this photograph. A doctor can find out whether there is illness in a patient's lungs and heart by listening through a stethoscope.

FACT BOX

• The great Indian physician (doctor) Susruta, first discovered that mosquitoes spread malaria and that rats spread plague 1,500 years ago.

• Doctor Willem Kolff invented the first artificial kidney machine in 1943. Like a kidney, the machine removes poisons from a person's bloodstream. People whose kidneys are too damaged to work use this machine.

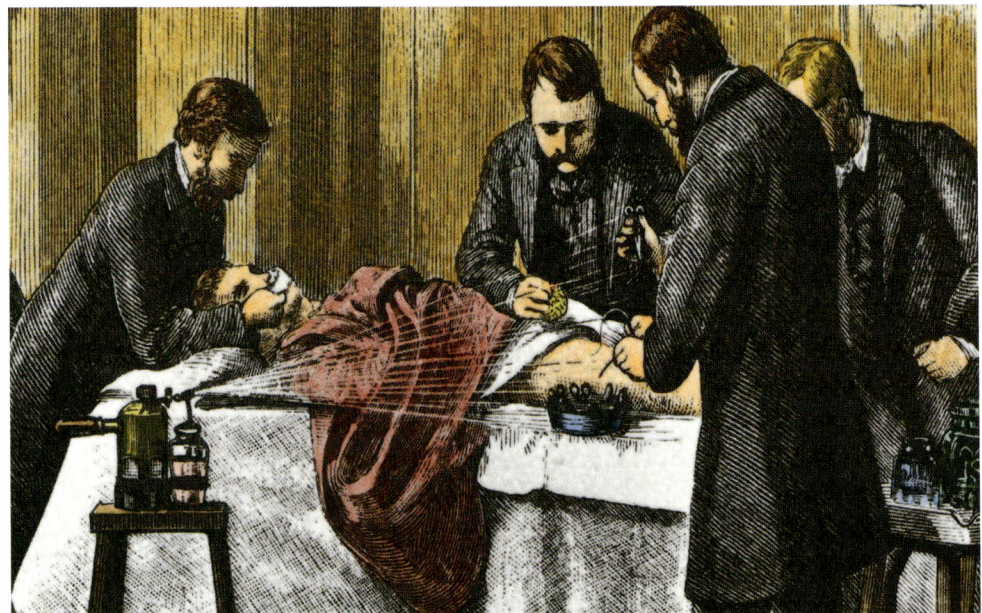

Keeping clean

Surgeons began to use carbolic sprays of the kind shown in this engraving whenever they operated on a patient. Far more people survived surgery because of this. Before the 1800s, many people died after surgery (cutting a body open) because germs infected open wounds. The British surgeon, Joseph Lister, invented a way of preventing this. He washed the wounds in carbolic acid, a chemical that kills germs.

ether inhaler

It's a knockout

When surgeons cut people open they are able to give them an anaesthetic (drug that puts people to sleep) to stop them feeling pain. The first modern anaesthetic was discovered in the USA by a dentist, William Morton. In 1846 he used the chemical called ether to stop a patient feeling pain from surgery. Ether inhalers, like the one shown here, were invented to allow patients to breathe in ether before and during an operation.

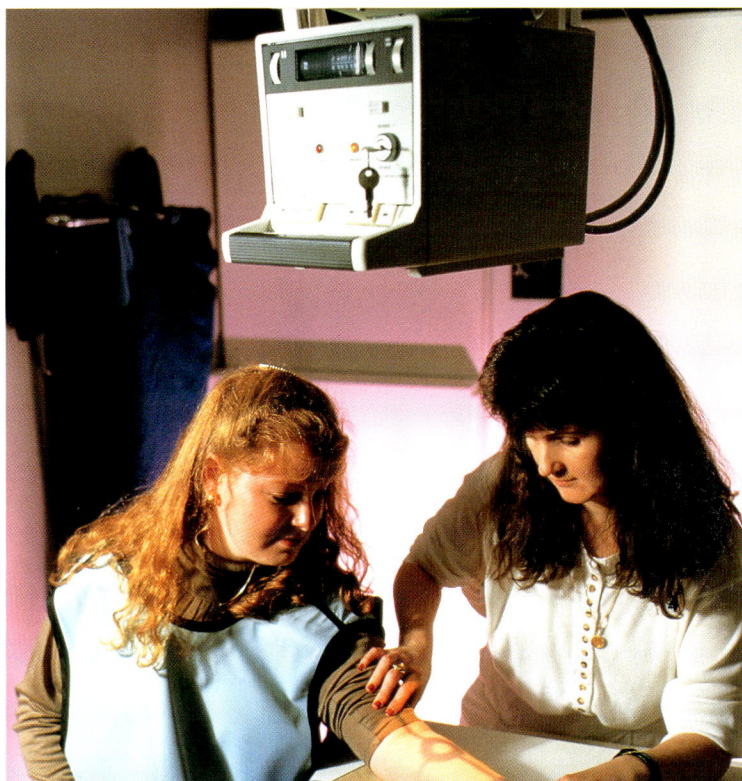

See-through machine

A radiographer (X-ray specialist) uses an X-ray machine to photograph bones inside a patient's arm. Radiation (radio waves that pass through the air) from the machine passes through the patient and strikes a piece of film leaving a picture of her bones. The German scientist Wilhelm Konrad von Röntgen discovered this special radiation by accident in 1895.

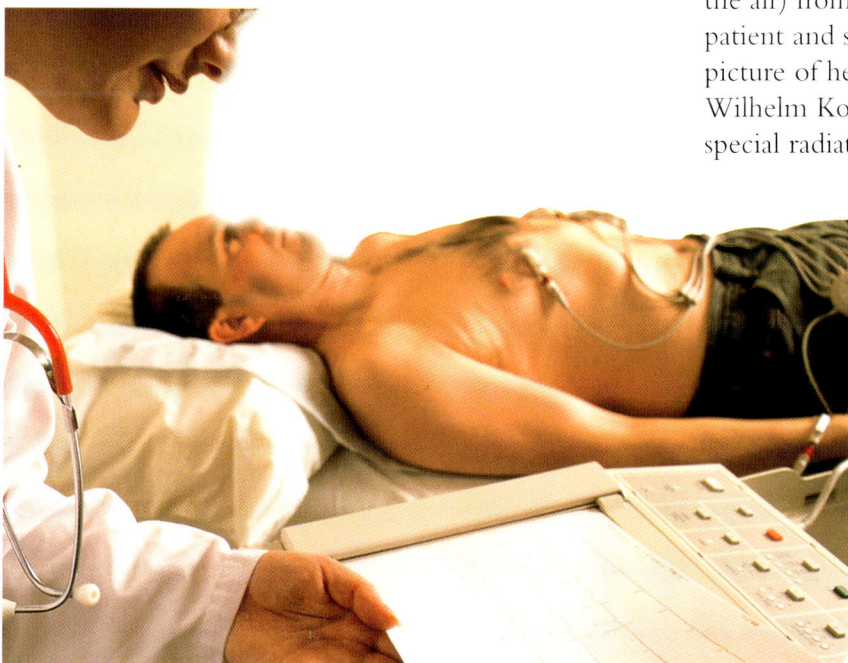

Just a pinprick

Many drugs are given by injecting them into a person's vein or muscle using a hypodermic syringe. Usable syringes were invented in the 1600s but they carried germs. In 1869 the French scientist Luer invented the first all-glass syringe. This was easier to keep germ-free. Disposable syringes became available in the 1970s.

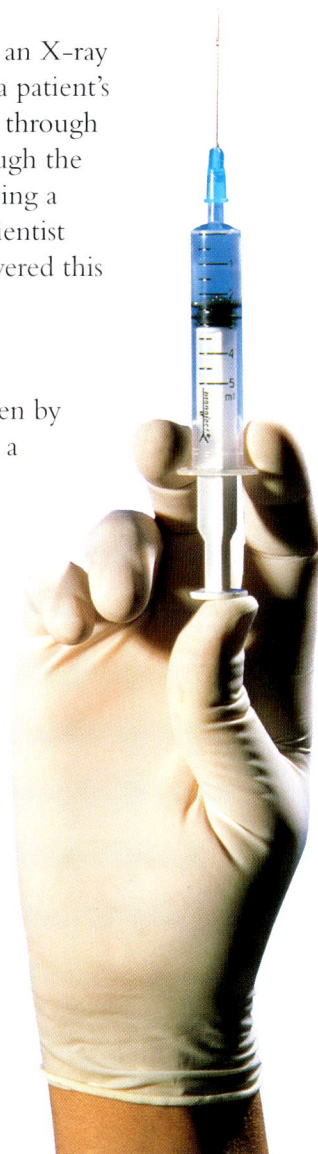

Beating heart

Modern electrocardiographs (ECGs) such as this one can be used in hospitals everywhere to check patients' heartbeats and warn of heart disease. The Dutch scientist Willem Einthoven invented a way of recording the beating of people's hearts as a line on a piece of paper in 1901. However, his machine was very large and heavy. He was awarded the Nobel Prize for his achievement in 1924.

POWER TO THE PEOPLE

All charged up
The Italian scientist Alessandro Volta shows his invention to the Emperor Napoleon. He invented an electirc battery and named it after himself. He used discs of copper and zinc piled above each other separated by cardboard discs soaked in salt water. When joined together, they produce an electric current.

DISCOVERING how to make electricity was one of the most important steps human beings made in using energy for heat, light and many other purposes. Before this discovery, people relied on coal and wood for heat and muscle power for most other work. The ancient Greeks knew that rubbing amber with cloth produces static electricity but they did not know why. From the 1700s, many scientists in Europe and the United States tried to understand how electricity works and how to generate it. It was not until the 1800s that real progress was made. In 1829 Joseph Henry in the USA invented the first true electric motor, a machine that could use electricity to turn moving parts such as wheels and belts. In the 1870s and 1880s in Britain, Sir William Siemens built the first electric railway and the first electric turbines (machines that make electricity by using water force). The age of electricity began in earnest in 1884. The first electric power station, designed by Thomas Edison, was built in New York. In the modern world electricity is used everywhere.

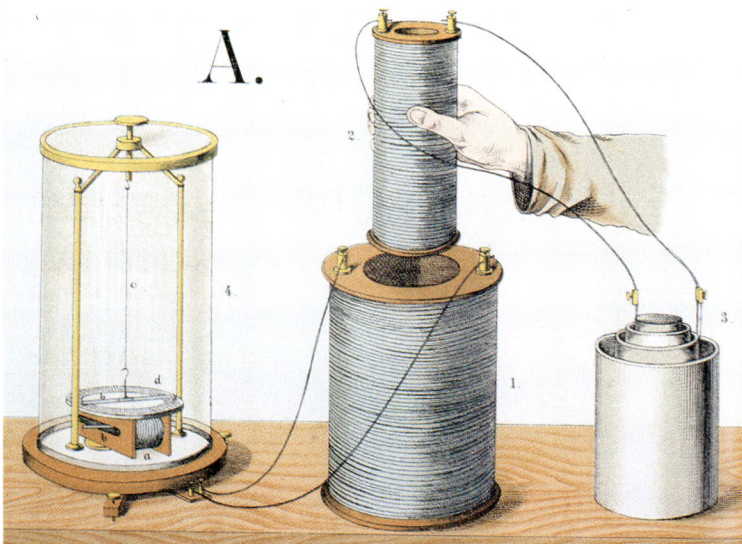

element

glass container

*Swan
electric lamp*

*electric
wires*

switch

Not a flicker
By the early 1800s scientists knew that passing electricity through a thin wire could make it heat up and give out light. But it took until the 1870s for Sir Joseph Swan and Thomas Edison to invent light bulbs that would light an ordinary room without quickly burning out. By the 1880s, the Swan electric lamp was being sold commercially (in shops).

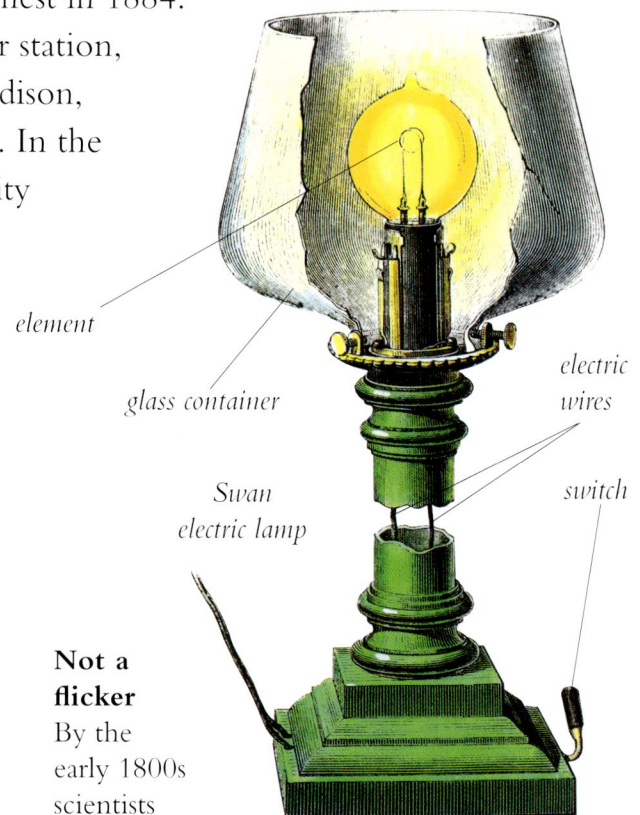

A.

Magnetic power
In 1831 Michael Faraday showed that a magnetic field could produce electricity. Since the 1700s, scientists had experimented to find out if this was possible. Faraday's device produced electricity using changes in the magnetic force of an iron wire. His discovery made it possible to build all later electric generators.

Bright as day

Electric power enabled work that needed good light, such as making detailed drawings, to be done at night. Before the electric light bulb was invented, people depended on candles, oil lamps and gas lights. They were inconvenient to use. The clear, steady light of electric light bulbs made work easier.

Six-bar sizzler

Electric fires make it very easy for us to warm up when it is cold. The first electric fires were invented in the late 1800s. This fire from the 1900s works in the same way as electric fires of today. Electricity warms up the wire which is coiled around the bars of the fire, to create heat.

1913 Belling electric fire

Power from the atom

A nuclear power station contains nuclear reactors that release energy which generates electricity. The potential of nuclear power was realized with the development of the atomic bomb in World War II. Making electricity from nuclear power is more expensive than using coal. The radiation from the nuclear waste is also very dangerous.

Razzle dazzle

Big cities are full of neon advertisements such as the flashing lights in Piccadilly Circus, London. In 1910, the French chemist George Claude sealed neon gas into a thin glass tube. He discovered that electricity made the gas give out a bright reddish-orange light. Soon after, ways were invented of using this brightly coloured light on the front of buildings to advertise goods.

CREATING ENERGY

ENERGY is needed to do work. Electrical power, steam power, and even horse power are all forms of energy. The two projects described here explore different ways in which energy can do work to make something move. The development of the steam engine and the electric motor in the 1800s provided completely new sources of energy. They used that energy to power ships and railway engines, for example, and to light homes and streets.

   The turbine project shows you how the energy of water pouring out of a bottle makes the bottle spin round and round. It is that kind of energy on a much bigger scale that turns turbines in power stations, so generating electricity. The electric motor project shows you how power from an electric battery can turn a cotton reel round and round. Electric motors are used in many household appliances such as vacuum cleaners and washing machines.

Reservoir power
This hydro-electric power station uses falling water to drive turbines that spin generators. The dam is built across a valley and stores water that comes from streams and rivers. Turbines and generators are inside the dam wall.

MAKE A TURBINE

You will need: *scissors, plastic drinks bottle, pencil, 2 wide drinking straws, plastic sticky tape, thin string, water.*

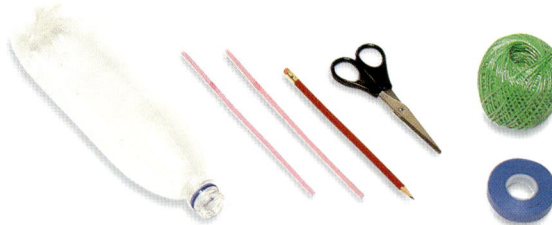

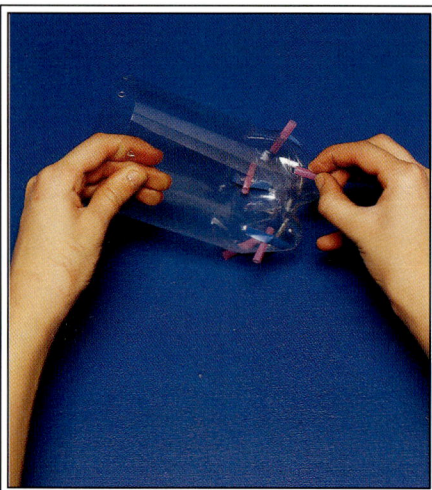

1 Cut off the bottle's top. Use the pencil to poke holes around its base. Cut the straws and push them through the holes. Use sticky tape to hold the straws to the bottle.

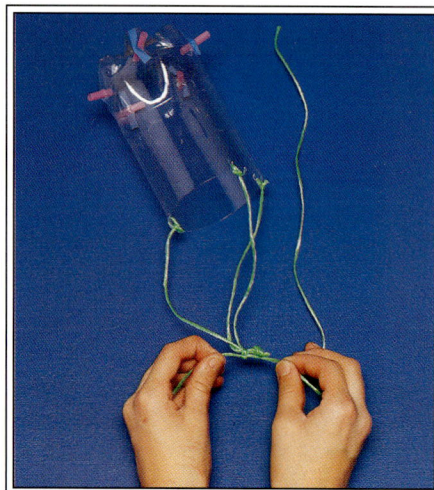

2 Poke three holes around the top of the bottle. Tie three equal lengths of string through the holes and join them to one long piece of string.

3 Hold your turbine over a tray or outdoors so the water will not make a mess. Fill the bottle with water. It squirts out through the straws, causing the bottle to spin.

MAKE AN ELECTRIC MOTOR

You will need: bradawl, ruler, plastic modelling board 5mm thick, (blue) base 15x10cm, 2 (red) end supports 5x5cm, 2 (yellow) coil supports, 6x5cm, 2 (white) coil support spacers 4x1cm, 2 (green) magnet supports 3cm high, glue suitable for sticking plastic, scissors, thin drinking straw, copper wire, aluminium kitchen foil, cotton reel, thin sticky tape, knitting needle 15cm long, 2 powerful bar magnets, 4 paper clips, 2 flexible connecting wires 20cm long, thick plastic sticky tape, 6 volt battery.

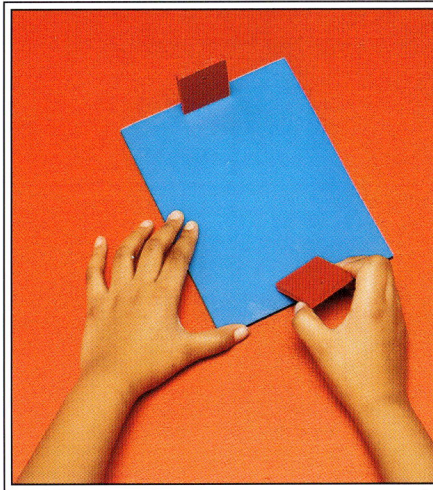

1 Use the bradawl to make a hole 1cm from the top of each of the two end supports. Glue them to the base board, 1cm inwards from the shorter edges.

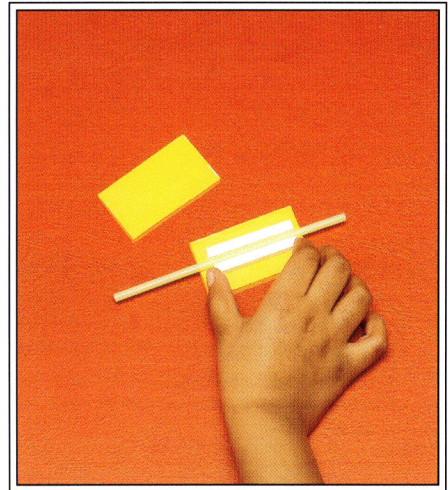

2 Cut a length of straw 12cm. Glue the straw to one coil support. Fix the two coil support spacers either side of the straw. Glue the second support over the top.

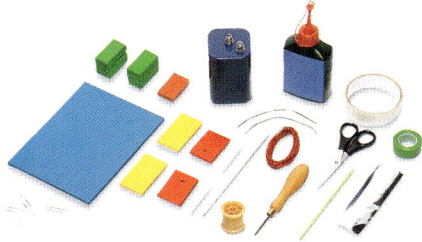

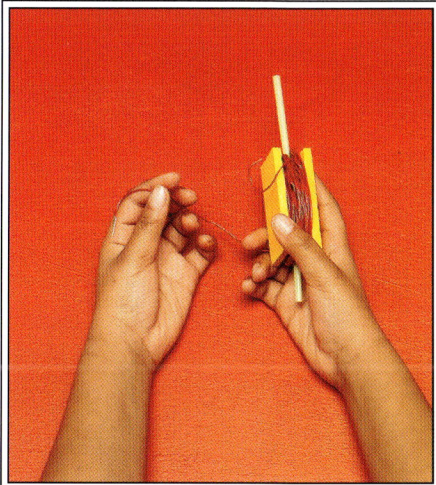

3 Strip 2cm of insulation from one end of the wire and 3cm from the other. Wind the wire tight between the coil supports. Slide the reel on to the straw. Cut a strip of foil the width of the reel.

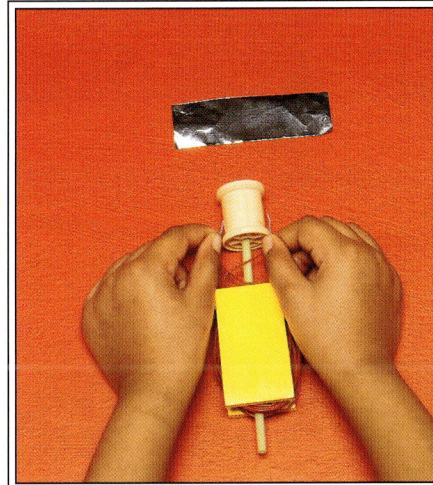

4 From this strip cut enough to fit three-quarters of the way around the reel. Cut it in half. Put the ends of the wire, which must not touch, against the reel. Tape a piece of foil over each wire so the wire is under the foil's centre.

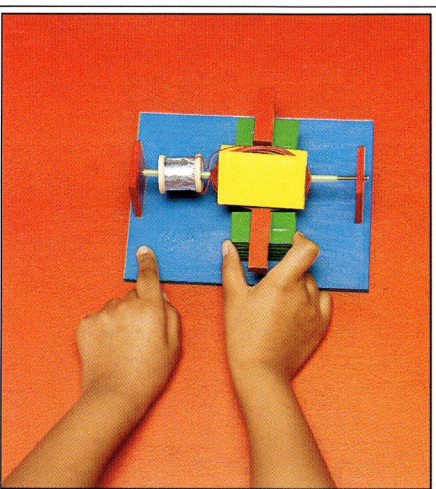

5 Stick the reel to the straw. Hold it between the end plates. Slide the knitting needle through the hole in each end plate. Secure the coil support with wooden blocks. Place the magnets on the supports so that the coil and reel spin freely.

6 Unbend two paper clips to make hooks. Join one end of each to a connecting wire and fix to the base with thick tape. Using paper clips, join the ends of the wires to the battery. The coil should start spinning round.

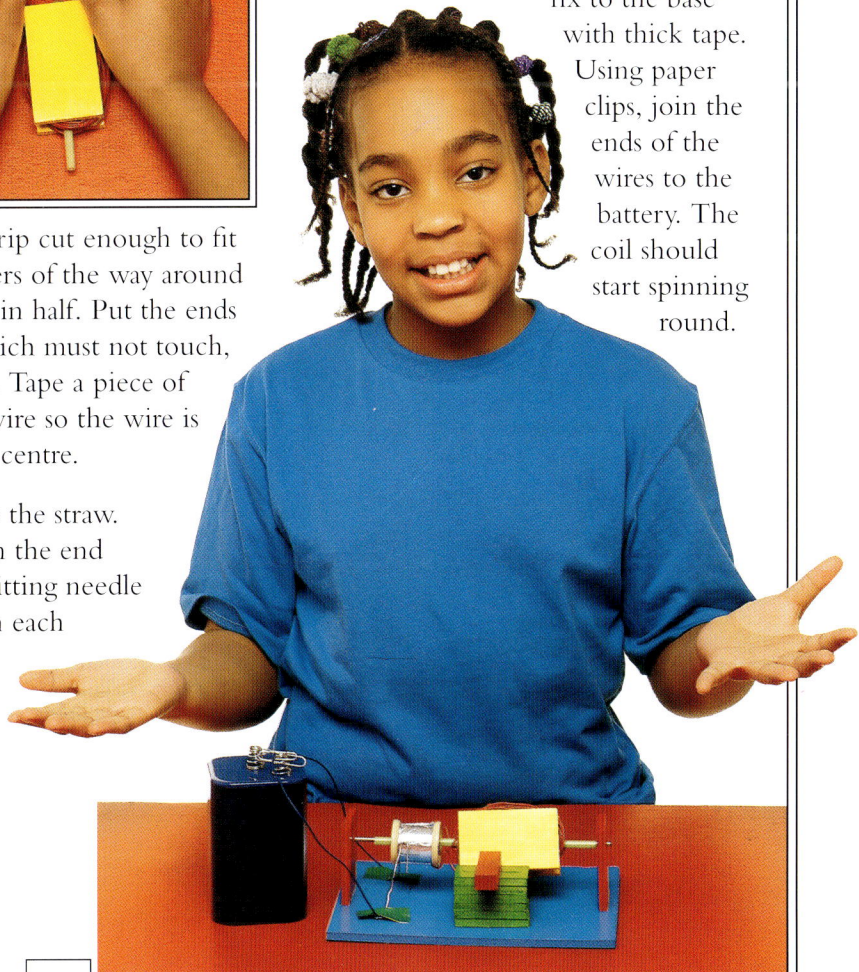

KEEPING IN TOUCH

IN the modern world, printed information is found in books, magazines, newspapers and downloaded from computers. None of these would exist without writing and alphabets or without the printing press. The first alphabets were invented between 5,000 and 3,500 years ago in the Middle East, India and the Mediterranean. The letters that make up the words in this book belong to the alphabet invented by the ancient Romans 2,500 years ago. The Romans borrowed and altered the ancient Greeks' alphabet.

Before they knew how to make paper, people in Europe wrote on wax tablets or sheets of parchment (animal skins) or carved words in stone and wood. The Chinese invented papermaking almost 2,000 years ago. The Arabs introduced paper to Europe in the 1100s. The Chinese also invented printing on paper about 1,000 years ago but Johannes Gutenberg invented both movable type (cut-out letters) and the printing press in the mid–1400s. Today, the most popular forms of communication are the telephone, e-mail and the Internet.

Written in stone
The ancient Egyptians had no alphabet. They used written signs called hieroglyphs such as these carved on stone, which illustrate people, animals and gods.

printing press

printed sheets

ink pad

Leaves of skin
Before printing, books in Europe were written by hand. They were often richly decorated. Pictures and writing were made with brushes and pens on parchment.

Read all about it
Johannes Gutenberg examines a page from the printing press that he invented. On the table is a pad for putting ink on the type. The type was made up into words and put under the press. The words were inked, a sheet of paper placed on top of them and the press squeezed down heavily.

Sharp instruments

The easiest way to write on parchment or paper is to use a long, thin instrument with a nib dipped in ink. For centuries, people used quills (sharpened goose or swan feathers) to write. By the 1800s, a way of making metal nibs, such as the one shown here, had been invented. These were much sharper and lasted far longer than quills.

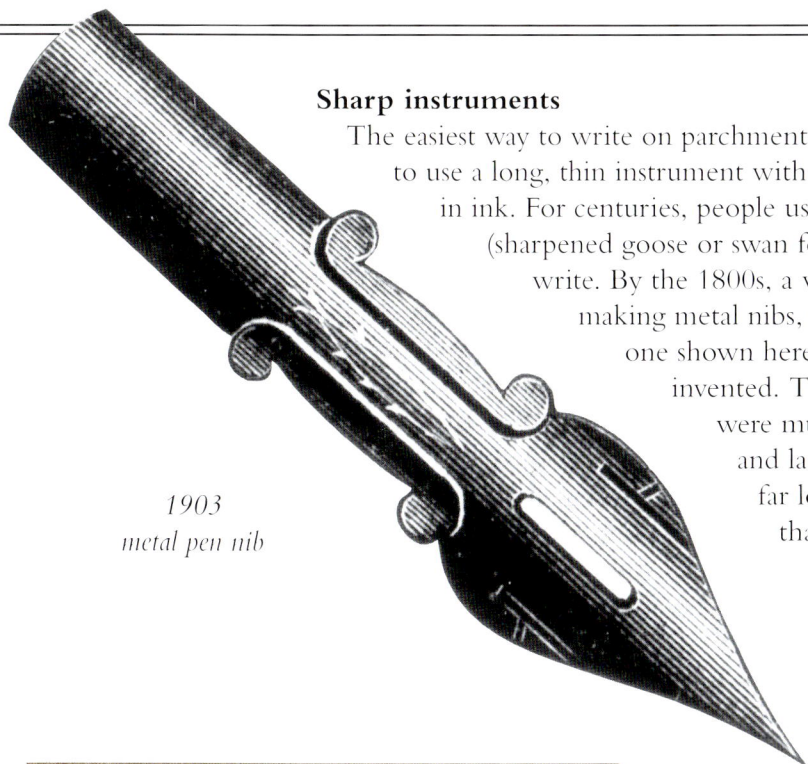

*1903
metal pen nib*

1924 telephone

Neat letters

Documents written on typewriters are easier to read than handwritten ones because the letter shapes do not change and the lines are evenly spaced. Christopher Sholes, the man who invented the first typewriter, was a printer who wanted to find a way to use type for writing rather than printing multiple copies. Sholes's daughter is shown here in 1872 using one of her father's experimental typewriters.

Long distance calls

The invention of the telephone by Alexander Graham Bell in 1876 opened up a new means of communication to people all over the world. Instead of writing to each other, they could simply pick up a telephone and talk. In the 1960s, telecommunication satellites were launched into orbit above the earth, making it easier and much cheaper to talk to people in other countries, often thousands of miles away.

ON THE WIRE

UNTIL about 200 years ago, the best way to send a message was to write a letter and give it to a rider on a fast horse. In 1838 the American, Samuel Morse, invented an electric telegraph that could send messages over a wire. Morse installed the first telegraph line between Washington and Baltimore in 1844. The first telegraph cable to span the Atlantic Ocean was laid in 1866. Some people have called the telegraph the Victorian Internet. Morse also invented a special code to use with his telegraph. The code is just like an alphabet, but instead of symbols there are long and short bursts of electricity that make blips of sound.

You can make your own telegraph and use it to communicate with a friend. There are two symbols used in telegraph communication, a dot (.) and a dash (-). Each letter of the alphabet is represented by a different group of dots and dashes.

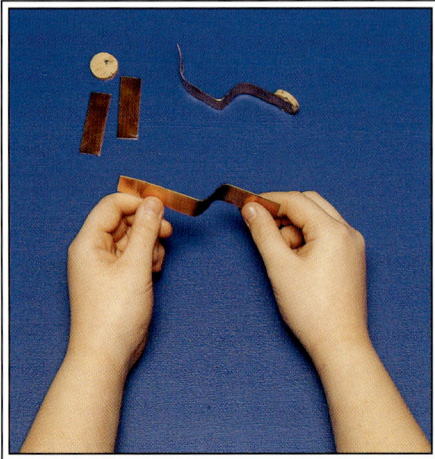

1 Cut 2cm from the end of each copper strip. Bend the longer strips to the shape shown here. Glue a circle of cork to one end.

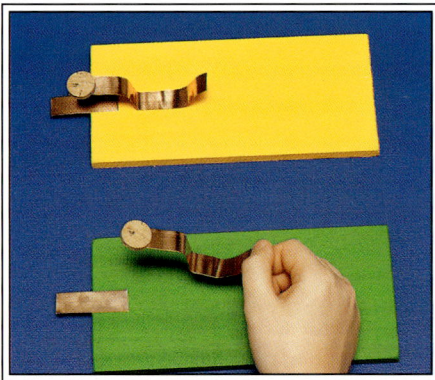

2 Use a drawing pin to fix a 2cm copper strip to each baseboard. Fix one copper strip with the cork to each of the baseboards. Position the cork just over the edge of the board.

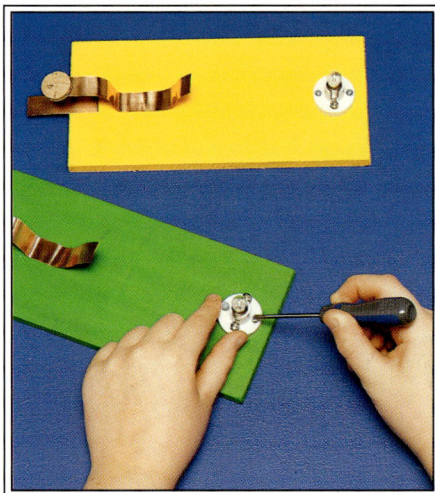

MAKE A TELEGRAPH

You will need: scissors, 2 flexible copper strips 10x1cm, strong glue, 2 cork circles, 4 drawing pins, 2 pieces of fibreboard 16x8cm, screwdriver, 2 bulb holders with screws to fix, 2 bulbs, 2 batteries with holders, 2 paper clips, plastic-covered wire.

3 Fix each bulb holder to the opposite end of the baseboard. Using a screwdriver, turn the screws clockwise to make them bite into the baseboard.

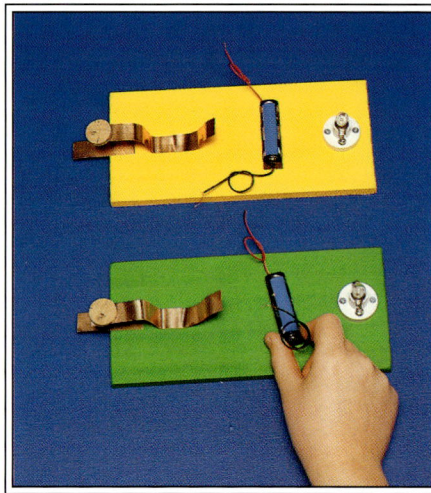

4 Glue a battery holder to each baseboard. Position it midway between the rear of the copper strip and the bulb holder. Remove 1cm of insulation from each of the wires.

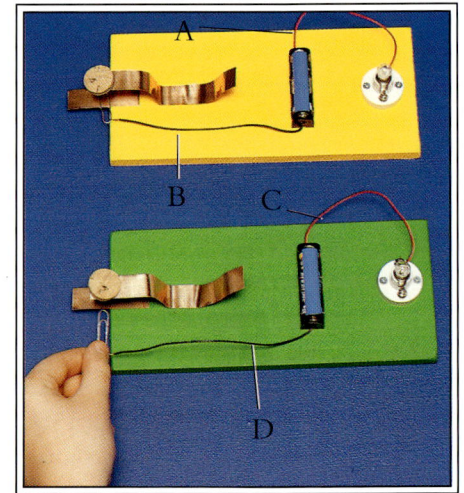

5 Attach the red wires (A and C) to the bulb screws as shown here. Attach the black wires (B and D) to the 2cm copper strip with a paper clip.

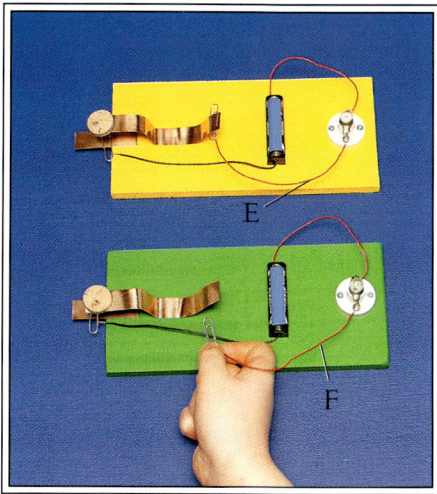

6 Use more wire to connect the rear end of each copper strip to one side of each bulb holder (wires E and F). Tighten the terminals on the holders to make a good connection.

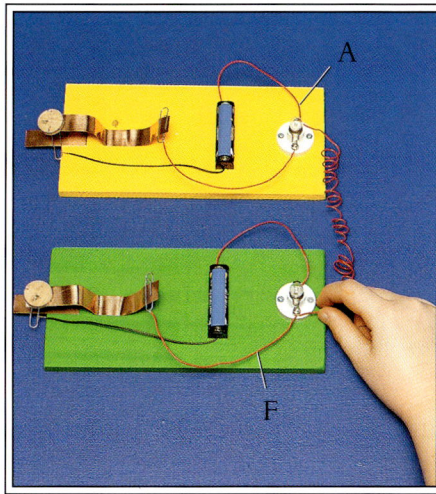

7 Using a length of wire at least a metre long connect wire A to wire F. Make sure the wires are tightly connected.

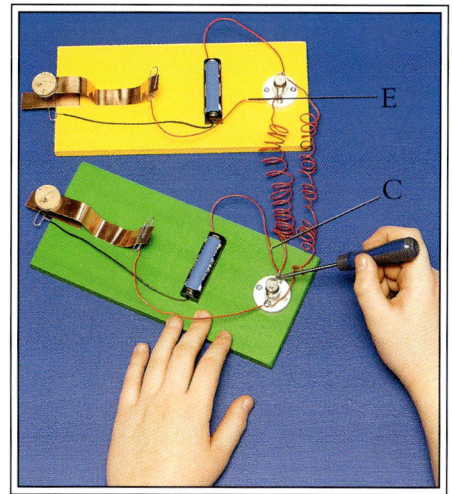

8 With an equal length of wire connect wire C to wire E as shown here. Again, make sure the wires are tightly conected.

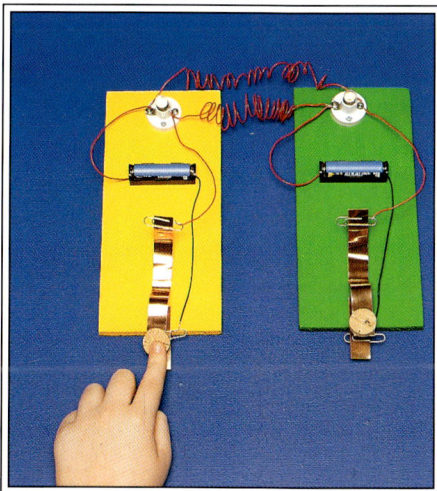

9 The telegraphs are now connected. Press one of the corks down to test whether your telegraph works. Both lights should light up.

10 To make a dash with your telegraph hold down the cork for half a second and to make a dot hold the cork down for a quarter of a second. Now you can try sending messages to a friend. Remember that your partner will have to look up each letter, so leave gaps when sending letters.

Slow talking

A telegraphist of the 1880s could send and receive about 80 letters of the alphabet each minute, which would be about 12 to 15 words a minute. You speak at the rate of about 200 to 300 words a minute.

WARNING!

Please take care when using electrical equipment. Always have an adult present.

WORLD OF SOUND

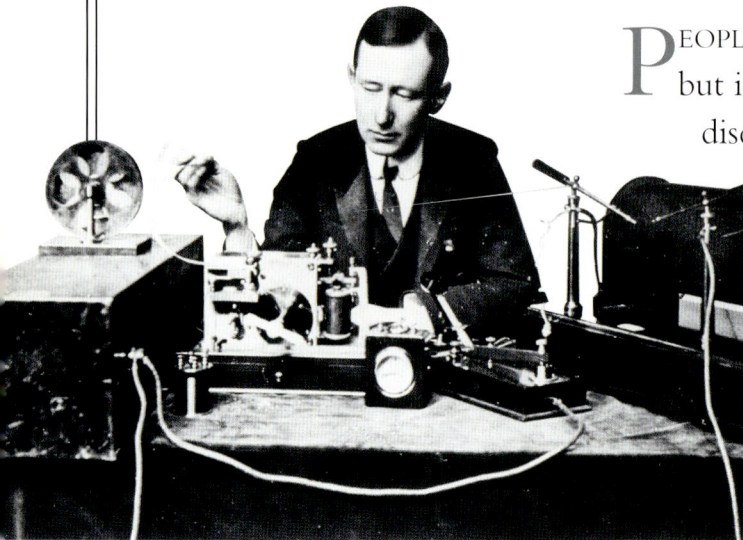

PEOPLE communicate by sound when they talk to one another, but if they are too far apart, they cannot hear each other. The discovery in the 1800s that it is possible to send sounds over long distances changed people's lives. It allowed them to speak to one another even though they were hundreds of miles apart. Sound can be carried long distances in two ways, along wires or through the air. When Alexander Graham Bell invented the first telephone in 1876, he used wires to send sound. Telephones continued to use wires for many years. In the late 1800s, the Italian Guglielmo Marconi invented a device that sent sounds through the air. It was called radio. Today people all over the world communicate by radio. In the 1800s, machines were also invented that allowed people to store sound so that it could be played back after it had been recorded. The first sound recorder, invented by Thomas Edison in 1877, was called a phonograph. In the mid-1900s, ways were invented to record sound on to tape and plastic compact discs (CDs).

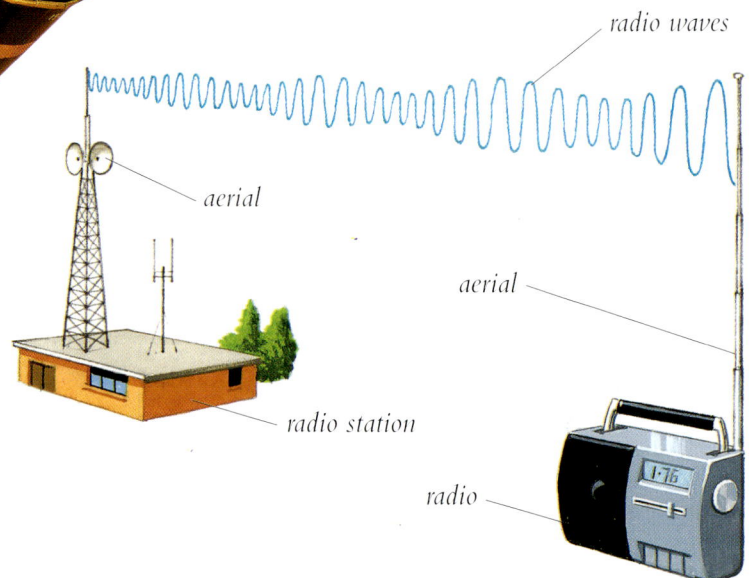

Radio genius
Guglielmo Marconi uses the radio equipment he invented. In 1901 he travelled to Newfoundland in Canada and there received the first transatlantic radio message. This proved that messages could be sent by radio over distances as great as the 4,800km between Europe and America.

Sound bites
On early phonographs such as this 1903 machine the sound was recorded on to a wax-coated cylinder. Each cylinder could only play for three to four minutes. In spite of this, phonographs became very popular.

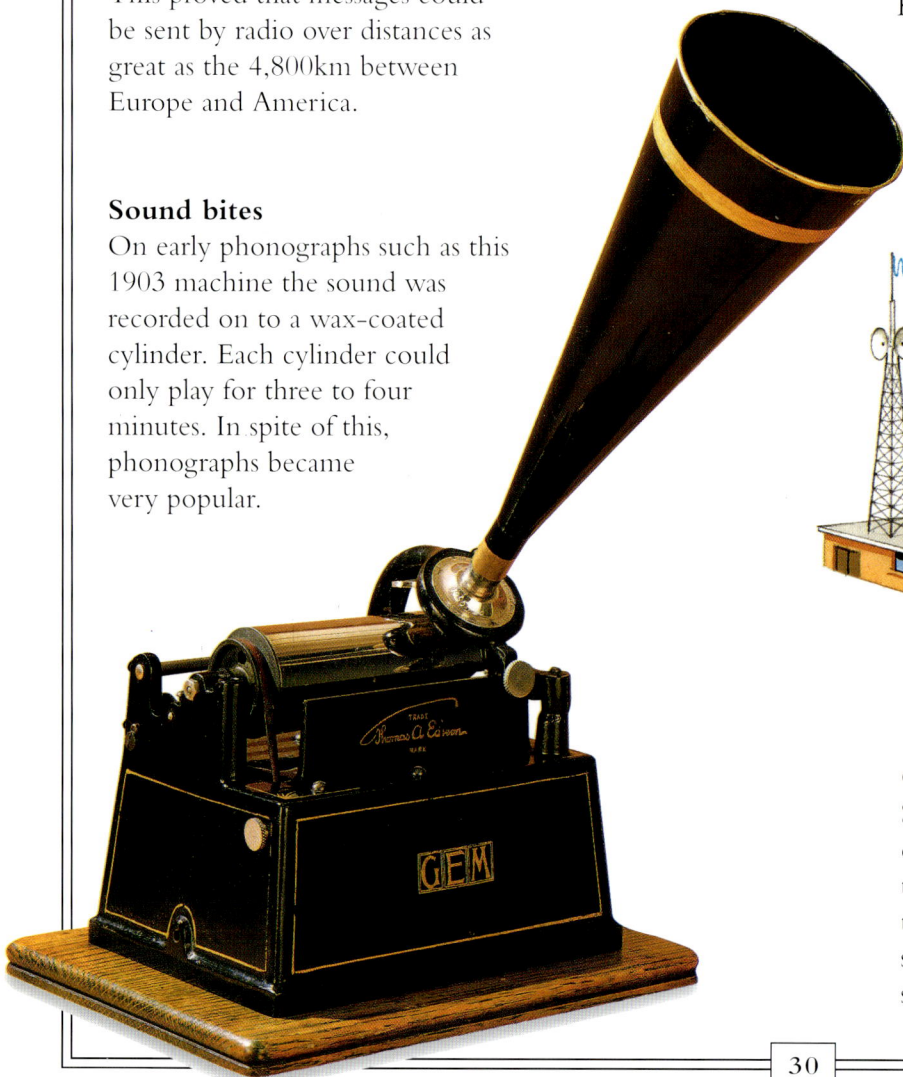

radio waves

aerial

aerial

radio station

radio

Carried on the air
Sounds such as the human voice are turned into electricity inside a microphone. The electric signal is then transmitted by an aerial as radio waves through the air. These waves travel to an aerial that passes the signal to a radio. The radio can be tuned to turn the signal back into sounds that people can hear.

Sound decorating

By the 1920s radios and speakers such as this were being made for use in the home. The radio, which was finished in a black textured metal case, was originally designed for use on polar expeditions. The speaker, however, was designed to be as beautiful as a piece of furniture.

The Golden Age

By the 1930s, radio had become an entertainment medium (a way of communicating) that broadcast news and music all over the world. People often called the radio the wireless because it was not joined to the transmitting station by wires. Millions listened in on radio sets, like the one shown here, to national radio networks such as the BBC in the UK and NBC in the USA.

Cool sounds

This type of radio became very popular in the 1950s. It used transistors, which are tiny electronic components that amplify (strengthen) weak radio signals. Transistor radios were also quite small and therefore portable. The transistor was invented in 1948 and is now used in many electronic devices.

Dramatically vivid discs

This DVD (Digital Video Disc) player offers a richness of sound and clarity of picture not previously available in other machines. Like a CD (compact disc) player, it uses a laser to scan across the surface of a plastic disc. The digitally recorded sounds on the disc are then fed into earphones through which the user listens.

LISTEN TO THIS

SOUND is energy that moves back and forth through the air as vibrations. These vibrations spread outwards as waves, like the ripples caused by a stone dropped into a still lake. Inventors have created ways to communicate by chanelling these sounds.

In the first part of this project, you can see how sound waves can be made to travel in a particular direction. Channelling the sound inside a tube concentrates the waves in the direction of the tube. By channelling sound towards a candle, you can use the energy to blow out the flame. The second part of this project shows how sound is a form of energy. Loud sounds carry large amounts of energy. Scientists say that loud sounds have large amplitudes (strengths). The last part investigates pitch (frequency of vibration). Low sounds consist of a small number of vibrations every second. Musicians say low sounds have low pitch but scientists say they have low frequency. You can make a set of panpipes and see how pitch depends on the length of each pipe.

Play it again, Sam!
You can play deep notes or low notes on a guitar. The sound waves vibrate slowly with a frequency as low as 50 times each second, high notes vibrate much more rapidly.

HOW SOUND TRAVELS

You will need: *clear film, tube of card, elastic band, candle, matches.*

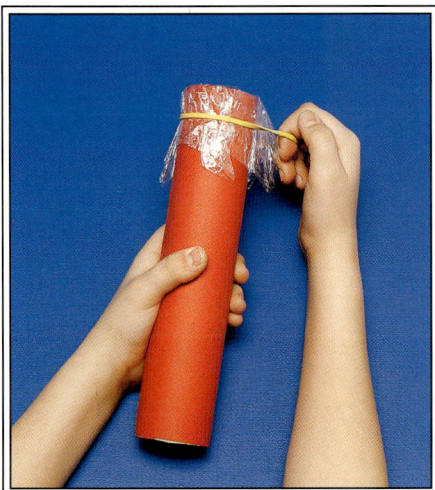

1 Stretch the clear film tightly over the end of the tube. Use the elastic band to fasten it in place. You could also use a flat piece of rubber cut from a balloon.

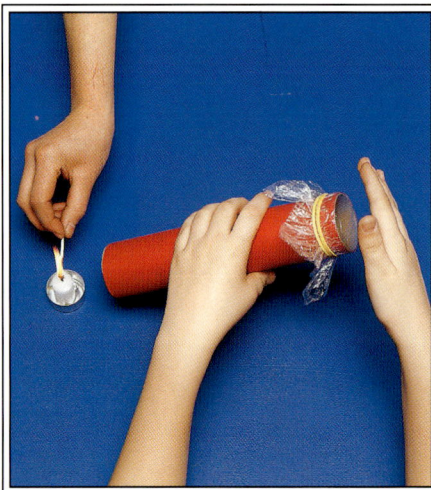

2 Ask an adult to light the candle. Point the tube at the candle, with the open end 10cm from the flame. Give the clear film a sharp tap with the flat of your hand.

3 You hear the sound coming out of the tube. It consists of pressure waves in the air. The tube concentrates the sound waves towards the candle flame and puts it out.

SOUND WAVES

You will need: clockwork watch, tube 5cm x 1m long.

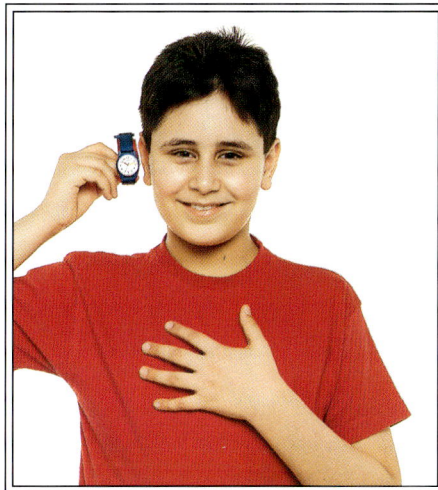

1 Place the watch close to your ear. You can hear a ticking sound coming from it. The sound becomes fainter when you move the watch away from your ear.

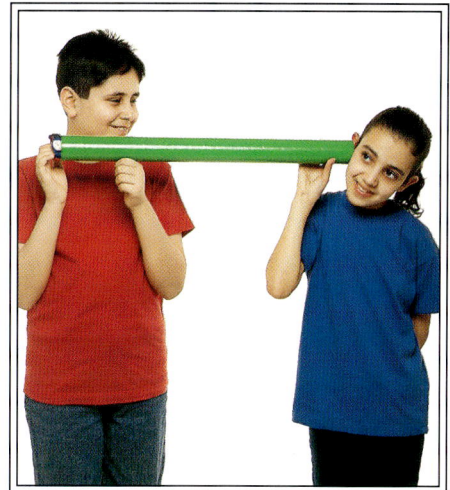

2 Place one end of the tube to a friend's ear and hold the watch at the other. The tube concentrates the sound and does not let it spread out. She can hear the watch clearly.

HOW TO MAKE PANPIPES

You will need: scissors, wide drinks straws, modelling clay, card, sticky tape.

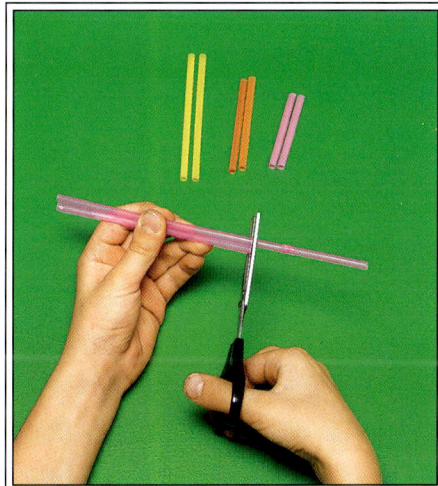

1 Cut the straws so that you have pairs that are 9cm, 8cm, 7cm, and 6cm long. Block one end of each straw with a small piece of modelling clay.

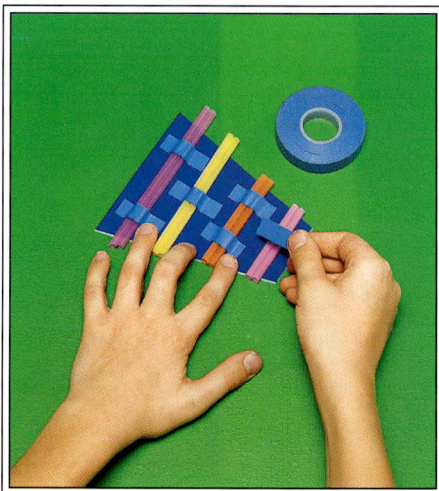

2 Carefully cut out the card to the same shape as the blue piece shown above. Tape the straws into place with the modelling clay along the most slanted edge.

3 Gently blow across the tops of the straws. You will find that the longer pipes produce lower notes than the shorter pipes. The longer pipes have a lower pitch and the shorter pipes have a higher pitch.

SEEING MORE

OVER the centuries, people have invented instruments that increase the power of the human eye. The microscope allows people to see very small things that are close to them. The telescope lets people see things that are very far away. Both microscopes and telescopes use lenses (specially shaped pieces of glass) to magnify the images that the eye sees. Spectacles help people with impaired vision to see clearly.

People knew 2,000 years ago that looking at something through a lens could magnify what they saw. At the beginning of the 1600s the Italian Galileo Galilei invented a tube with two lenses placed in it that allowed him to see details of the surface of the Moon. This was the first telescope. Later in the same century, Robert Hooke in England and Antoni van Leeuwenhoek in Holland invented the first microscopes. Since then microscopes and telescopes have become more and more powerful. By the end of the 1900s, telescopes had been built that can let us see stars trillions of kilometres away. Microscopes now exist that let us see creatures as tiny as germs.

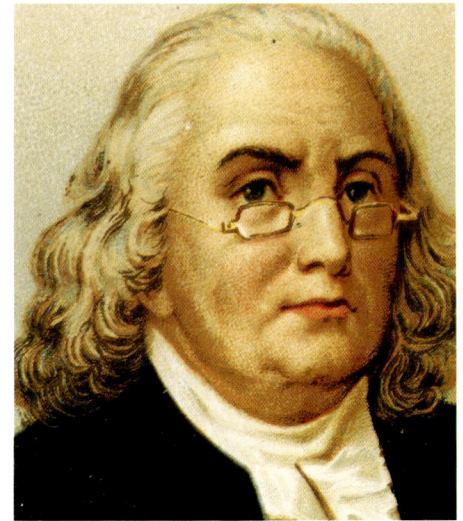

Double vision

In the 1700s Benjamin Franklin, the American statesman, writer and scientist, invented bifocal spectacles. Bifocals are two lenses combined into one. They enable people to see clearly at both short and long distances.

Looking closely

This is one of the first microscopes ever made. It was invented in the 1600s by the English scientist, Robert Hooke. Through it he could see tiny objects such as the cork cells shown in the book on the left. Hooke shone light through the glass globe on the right to light up the objects he looked at through the microscope.

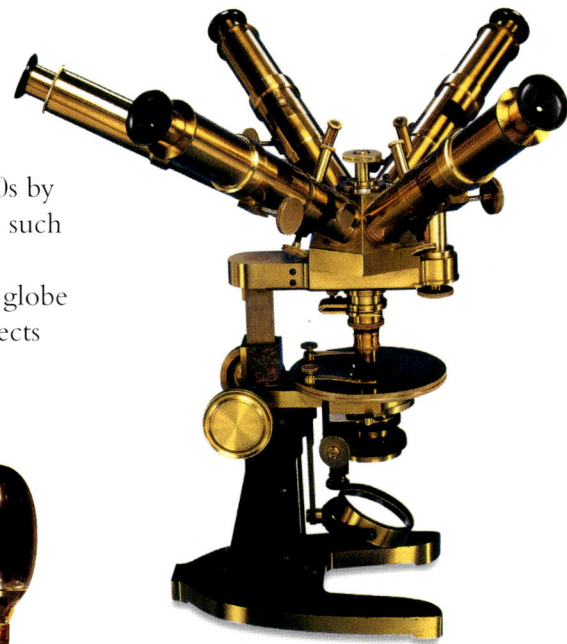

picture of cork cells

microscope

light focused through globe

Fivefold vision

Doctors soon used microscopes so that they could see the human body's parts in great detail. This microscope, invented in the 1800s, has five barrels to allow five different people to look through it at the same time. It was used in medical schools.

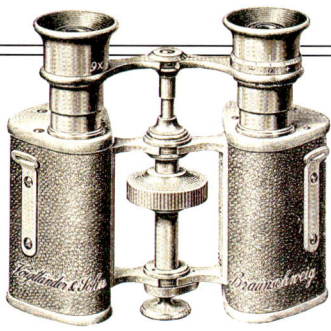

double barrelled

Binoculars such as these were invented in the early 1800s. Like telescopes, they use lenses to make distant objects seem closer but have two barrels rather than one. People using binoculars look through both barrels. Binoculars are shorter and easier to carry around than telescopes.

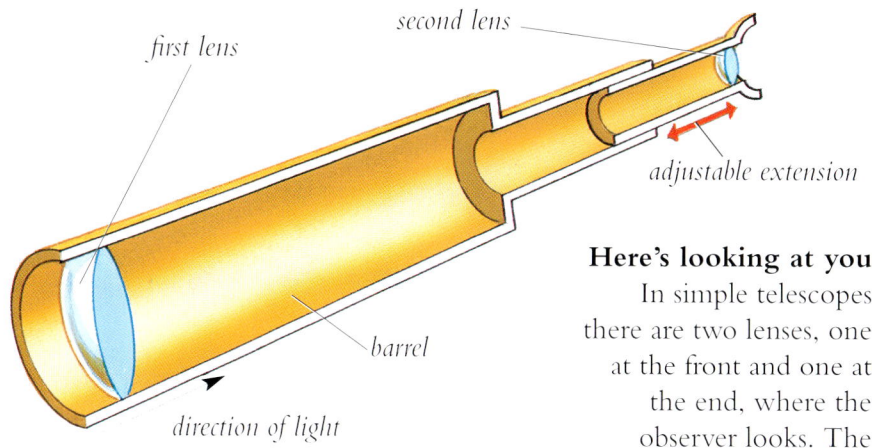

first lens

second lens

adjustable extension

barrel

direction of light

Here's looking at you

In simple telescopes there are two lenses, one at the front and one at the end, where the observer looks. The front lens concentrates the light that shines through it and turns the image upside down. The lens at the other end concentrates the light more and magnifies the image still further.

Stargazer

When the Italian scientist Galileo Galilei learned in the early 1600s of a telescope invented in Holland he decided to make one for himself. He had soon built a telescope through which he could clearly see the craters on the surface of the Moon. Galileo's telescope allowed him to discover the four largest of the moons around the planet Jupiter, 600 million km from Earth. The telescope to the right of Galileo's was invented by Sir Isaac Newton in the late 1600s.

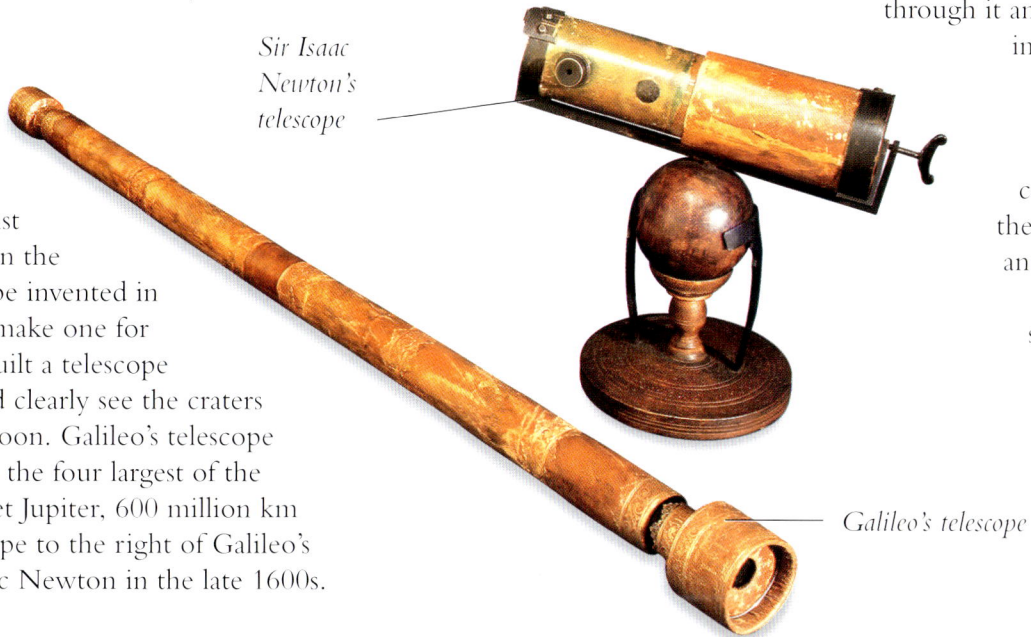

Sir Isaac Newton's telescope

Galileo's telescope

FACT BOX

• The largest mirror used in a telescope is at the Mount Palomar Observatory in California, USA. The mirror is 5m wide and allows those using the telescope to see for enormous distances deep into space.

• Electron microscopes allow people to see objects as tiny as the individual cells that make up our bodies. These microscopes do not use lenses but beams of electrons (electrically charged particles).

Orbiting observatory

The Hubble space telescope was launched into space in 1990. It orbits the Earth at a distance of 600km. Instead of lenses, it uses mirrors that move to see the stars. The first telescopes like this were invented in the 1600s. The Hubble telescope is much bigger than those. The larger of its two mirrors is 2.4m wide.

BLOW UP

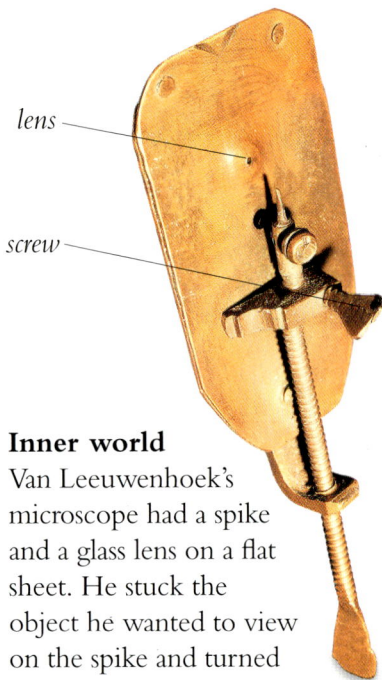

lens

screw

Inner world
Van Leeuwenhoek's
microscope had a spike
and a glass lens on a flat
sheet. He stuck the
object he wanted to view
on the spike and turned
the screw to bring the object
opposite the lens. Then he
turned the microscope over and
looked through the lens.

THE earliest microscope was invented by the Dutch scientist Antoni
van Leeuwenhoek around 1660. It contained a single round glass lens
about the size of a raindrop.

If you look at an ordinary magnifying glass you will see that the two
surfaces curve slightly. The curved surfaces bend light as it travels from the
object to your eye. A window pane has two flat surfaces and so does not
act as a magnifying glass. Powerful magnifying glasses have highly curved
surfaces. Van Leeuwenhoek realized that a glass sphere has the maximum
possible curvature. As a result, a spherical lens has the maximum possible
magnification of about 300 times. The invention of this microscope
opened up a whole new world. For the first time, people could see pollen
grains from flowers, bacteria and the sperm from male animals. In this
project you can make a copy of van Leeuwenhoek's microscope by using
a tiny droplet of water instead of a glass sphere.

JAM JAR MICROSCOPE

You will need: *two large jam jars,*
water, a pencil.

2 Find the
position that
gives the clearest
image with the
greatest
magnification.

4 You will find
that the image
is about four or
five times larger
than before.

1 Fill a jam jar with water and
place it at the edge of a table.
Look through the jar with one eye
and move the pencil back and forth
behind the jam jar.

3 Place a second water-filled jam
jar close behind the first one.
Hold the pencil in the water in the
second jar. Move the pencil back
and forth.

WATER DROP MAGNIFIER

You will need: *aluminium milk bottle cap, metal spoon, candle, small nail, water, flower.*

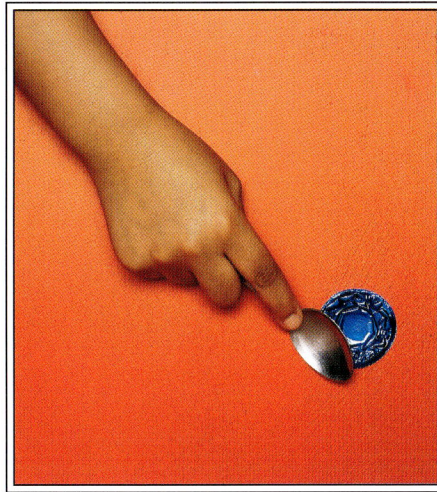

1 Place the milk bottle cap on a hard surface. Use the outer bowl of a spoon to flatten the cap. Stroke the spoon from side to side until the centre of the cap is flat and smooth.

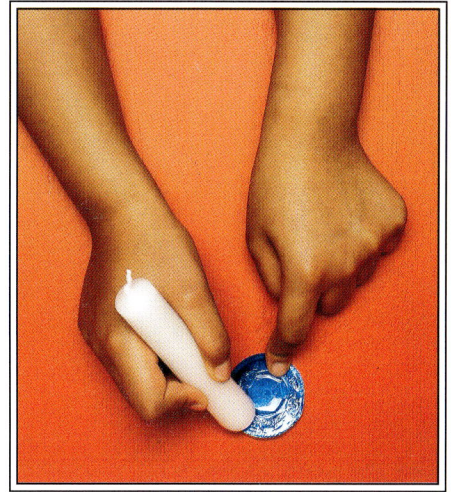

2 Rub the milk bottle cap on both sides with the end of a candle. Make certain that both sides of the smooth centre part are coated with a thin layer of wax.

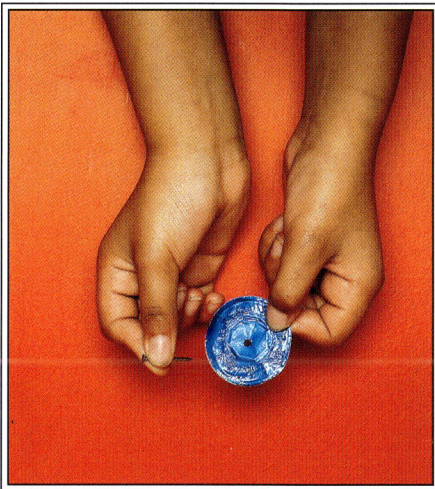

3 Push the nail through the centre of the milk bottle cap to make a small hole in it. The hole should be perfectly round and measure about 2mm across.

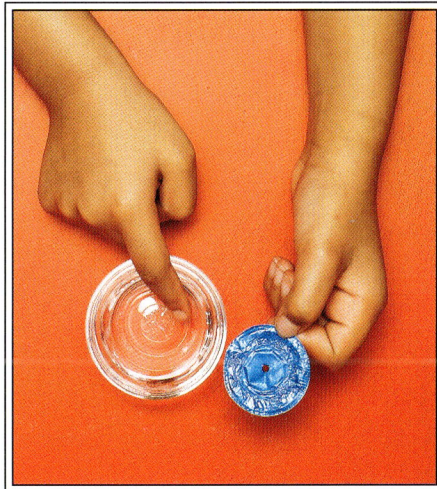

4 Collect water on a fingertip so that a droplet hangs down. Hold the cap flat and lower the drop on to the hole. The wax holds the water in a round lens shape.

5 To use your magnifier, hold it about 1 to 2cm from the object. Now bring your eye as close to the water droplet as possible. Look at how the flower is magnified.

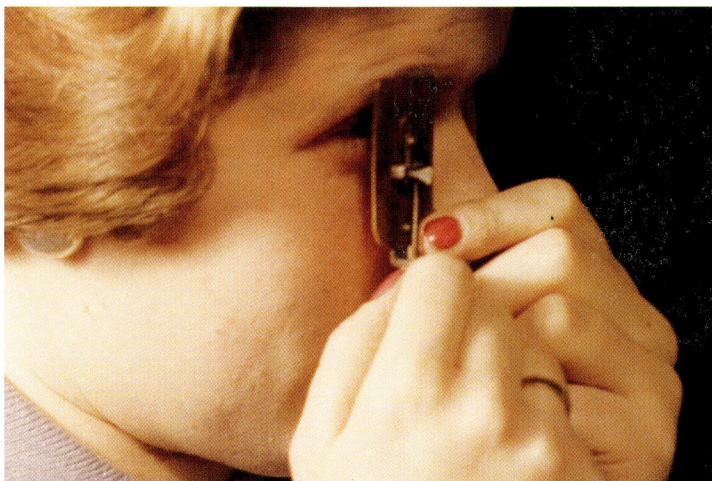

The world in a grain of sand
This woman is using van Leeuwenhoek's simple microscope by pressing it against her eye. Unlike most later microscopes, this was not a heavy instrument which could not be moved easily but a light, portable object. By using this microscope scientists were able to discover much more about the world around us, including the insides of our own bodies.

PICTURE SHOWS

Box of tricks
This early camera was so large and cumbersome that the user needed a handcart to carry it in. The extra equipment is for developing the photographs. This camera dates from the 1850s.

A SIMPLE form of photography began almost 2,000 years ago. The ancient Greeks discovered that light passing through a small hole in the wall of a dark room would make an image in the room of what was outside. In the 1500s, scientists discovered the same happened if a tiny hole was made in a completely dark room. They called the room a *camera obscura*. In the early 1800s scientists tried to find a way to permanently record the image this box made. If they were successful, it would mean that they could make pictures of the world without drawing or painting. The scientists put lenses into their cameras to sharpen the image. In 1840 William Fox Talbot invented a way of coating paper with light-sensitive chemicals that recorded the camera's image permanently.

By the late 1800s Thomas Edison had invented a camera that could record motion, and a kinetoscope, a machine that could project moving pictures. By the beginning of the 1900s, motion pictures were being made and shown commercially. Now cinema is one of the biggest forms of entertainment in the world.

Silver light
Photographs like this portrait of the English inventor Michael Faraday with his wife were made in the mid-1800s. They are known as daguerrotypes after their inventor, Louis Daguerre. They were made on small sheets of copper coated with a light-sensitive layer of silver.

Positive outlook
The images in most cameras are made on to negatives. From these, the positives (the prints) are made. Using negatives means many prints can be made from one negative. The Polaroid camera shown here was invented in the 1940s. It was called an instant camera because it produced a positive image immediately.

Polaroid camera

Freeze-frame gallops

The first accurate photographs of an animal in motion were taken by the English photographer Eadweard Muybridge. While in California in 1877, Muybridge was asked by a horse trainer to take pictures of a racehorse. The trainer wanted to prove for a bet that all four of a galloping horse's legs came off the ground at the same time for a split second during the gallop. As these photographs show, the trainer was correct.

The full works

Two French brothers, Auguste and Louis Lumière, invented this camera for moving pictures in 1895. It was both a camera and a projector and so was much better than Edison's early kinetoscope. The brothers called their invention a *cinématographe*, which has given us the modern word cinema.

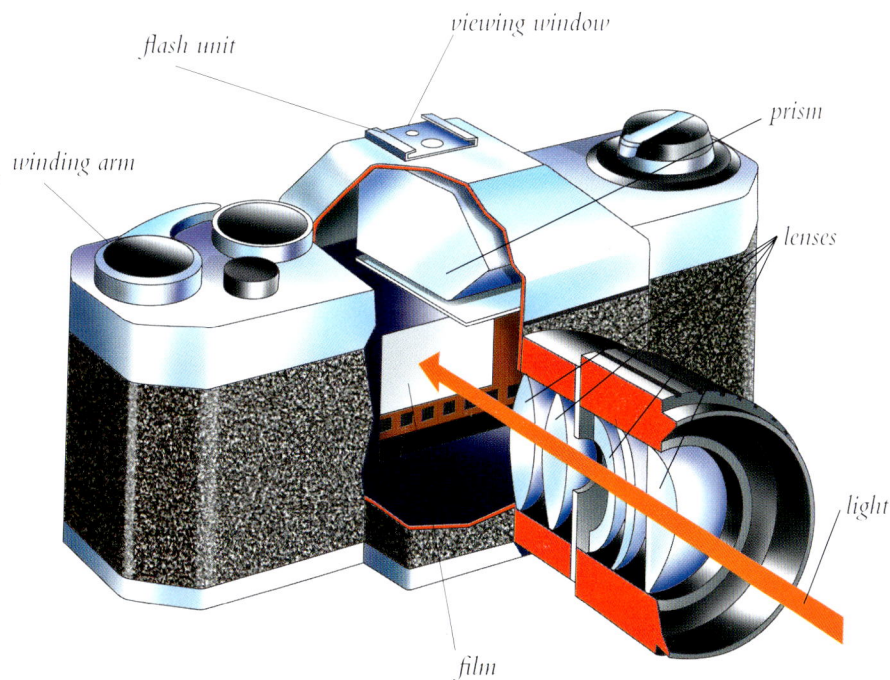

cinématographe

flash unit

viewing window

prism

winding arm

lenses

light

film

Picture by numbers

Digital cameras receive light through a lens in the same way as ordinary cameras. The difference in a digital camera is that the light, instead of striking a piece of plastic film, is digitally recorded by light sensors. The digital information is then stored inside the camera and can be played back on a computer screen.

Reflex action

Single lens reflex (SLR) cameras became very popular after they were first developed in the 1930s. Light enters the camera through the lenses at the front and strikes the negative at the back. Users can see clearly what they are photographing by means of a prism mounted in the camera.

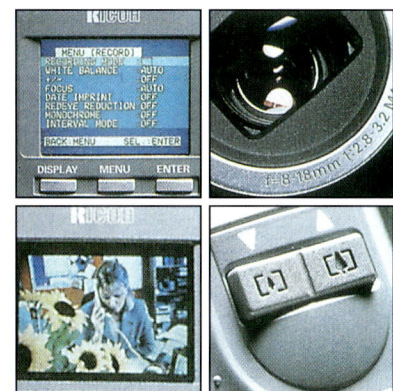

WINDOW ON THE WORLD

ONCE Guglielmo Marconi had invented a way to broadcast sound and people became interested in radio, inventors soon tried to find a way to broadcast pictures. John Logie Baird, a Scottish inventor, set himself the task of achieving this. Unfortunately no one else believed it was possible to broadcast pictures and he was forced to work alone and in great poverty.

In 1926, Baird finally succeeded in sending a picture a few metres, but his way of sending pictures was not perfect. In the 1930s Vladimir Zworykin, a Russian electrical engineer, invented a better way to send pictures by using electricity to run through a cathode ray tube. Zworykin's invention was essential for modern television. The first public television programmes were broadcast by the BBC in Britain in 1936, and by the 1950s, televisions were beginning to appear in every home in the United States and Europe.

dummy

disc

electric motor

Spinning circle
The first picture to be captured as electrical impulses was a dummy's head. Baird placed three discs with holes in them in front of the dummy. These created flashing patterns of light that were turned into electrical impulses by a photoelectric cell (device for turning light into electricity).

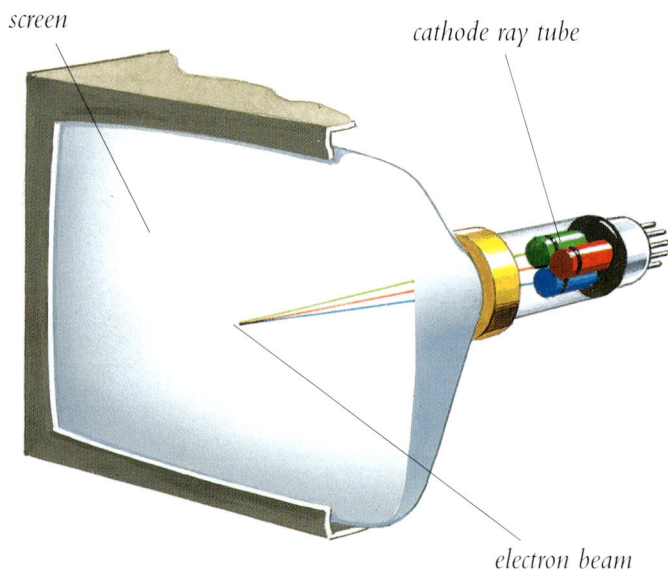

screen

cathode ray tube

electron beam

Tube travel
The cathode ray tube is the heart of a television. Pictures are received by the aerial in the form of electrical impulses. These impulses control a stream of electrons inside the cathode ray tube. The electron beam scans across the screen and creates the picture as points of coloured light. This is the picture that the viewer sees.

Box in the corner
The televisions that large numbers of people first began to buy in the 1950s looked very much like this one. The screens were small and the pictures could only be seen as black–and–white images. Reception was also difficult because there were very few transmitters.

1950s television

Light in the gloom

When television was first widely broadcast, people saw it as something very new. Most programmes were broadcast only in the evenings and families gathered together to enjoy this new form of entertainment. Gradually more and more people bought televisions.

Moving eye

The cameras used in modern television studios are much more complicated devices than John Logie Baird's invention. This camera is on wheels and can move around the people or objects being filmed. It can move in closer and tilt up or down. Inside the camera, the image is changed into electrical impulses.

Super cool

Modern television screens are much bigger than those available in the 1950s and most are in colour. Flat-screen televisions, such as this one, first became available in the early 1990s. These televisions do not have cathode-ray tubes. Liquid crystals display the picture on the screen.

SCREEN SCENES

THE picture on a television screen is made up from thin lines of light. Follow the instructions in this project and you will also see that the picture consists of just three colours - red, green and blue. Viewed from a distance, these colours mix to produce the full range of colours that we see naturally around us. A TV picture is just rows of glowing dots of coloured light. Fax machines work in a similar way to TV, only more slowly. Feed a sheet of paper into a fax machine and a beam of light moves back and forth across it. Dark places absorb the light and pale places reflect it. The reflected light enters a detector that produces an electric current. The strength of the current depends on the intensity of the reflected light. The electric current is changed into a code made up from chirping sounds that travel down the line to the receiving fax machine. The code controls a scanner that moves across heat-sensitive paper and produces a *facsimile* (copy) of the original. The last part of this project shows how a fax machine breaks an image into tiny areas that are either black or white.

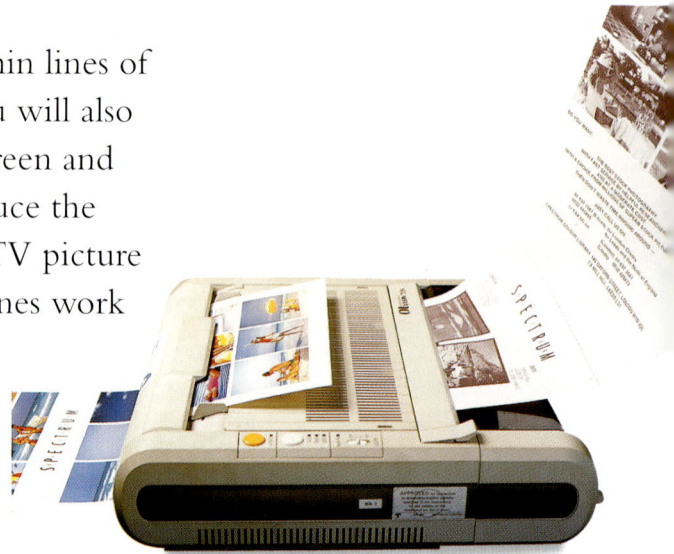

Fast messages
A fax machine sends pictures or writing down the phone line to another fax machine in seconds. The first fax machine was invented in 1904 by the German physicist Arthur Korn. They became common in the 1980s but they are slowly being replaced by electronic e-mail.

LOOKING AT A TV PICTURE

You will need: TV set, torch, powerful magnifying glass.

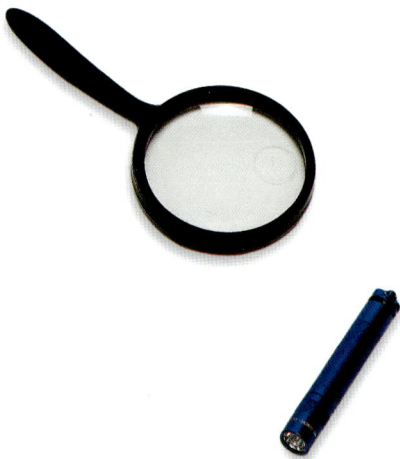

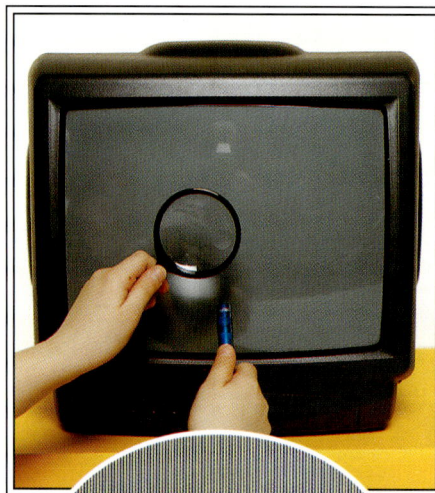

1 Turn off the TV. Shine the torch close to the screen and look through the magnifying glass. You will see that the screen is covered in very fine lines.

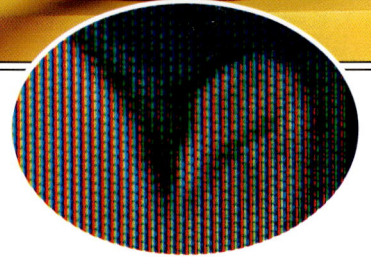

2 Turn on the TV and view the screen through the lens. The picture is made up of minute rectangles of light coloured red, green or blue.

Brand-new material

In the early 1900s, the chemist Leo Baekeland invented a way of creating a thick liquid from chemicals which, when it hardened, became a new material that no one had ever seen before. He called this material Bakelite. It was long lasting and could be shaped to make many different kinds of objects such as this radio case.

Strong and light

In the late 1800s, the electrolytic cell was invented as a way of using electricity to extract the light, strong metal called aluminium from bauxite ore. Aluminium is used when strong, light metal is needed, for example in building aircraft.

Riding on air

When motor cars were invented in the late 1800s their wheels were hard, like cartwheels. Charles Goodyear invented a process that made rubber hard and allowed people to make car tyres from it. Inside the tyres were inner tubes filled with air, which were first invented in 1845 by Robert Thomson.

CHEMICAL CHANGE

DURING the past 100 years, scientists have invented many substances that we take for granted today. Examples include plastics, medicines, detergents and fuels. These new substances are created by mixing natural substances that react to each other. These are called chemical reactions. There are just three main ways in which chemical reactions can happen: passing electricity through substances, heating them or mixing them together.

These experiments show the three ways in which chemical reactions can happen. In the first project, electricity breaks down salty water to make chlorine which is a disinfectant used to keep swimming pools clean. In the second project, you heat sugar, which is made from carbon, hydrogen and oxygen to create pure carbon. The third shows how to make the gas used in some fire extinguishers. This gas is made by mixing bicarbonate of soda and vinegar together to create carbon dioxide.

Measuring up
In a laboratory, this scientist is carefully measuring the exact amount of chemicals to add to a test tube in which the experiment will take place. In science, accuracy is very important.

ELECTROLYSIS

You will need: screwdriver, battery (4–6 volts), bulb and holder, wire, 2 paper clips, jar, water, salt.

WARNING!
Please take care when using electrical equipment. Always have an adult present.

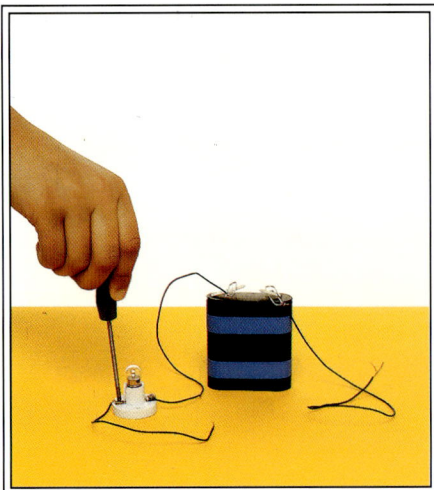

1 Connect the battery and bulb holder with wires as shown here. Remove 1cm of insulation from each end. Use the paper clips to join the wires to the battery.

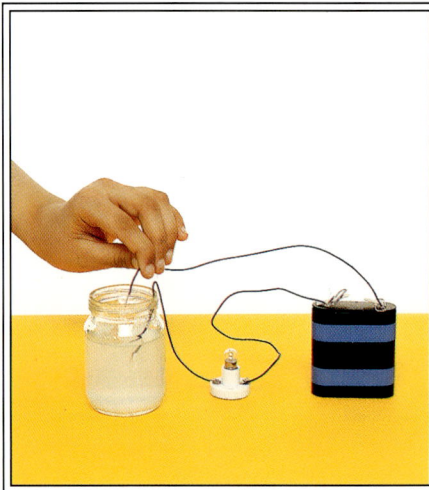

2 Stir salt into a jar of water until no more dissolves. Dip the two bare wire ends into the mixture and hold them about 1cm apart. Look for bubbles forming round them.

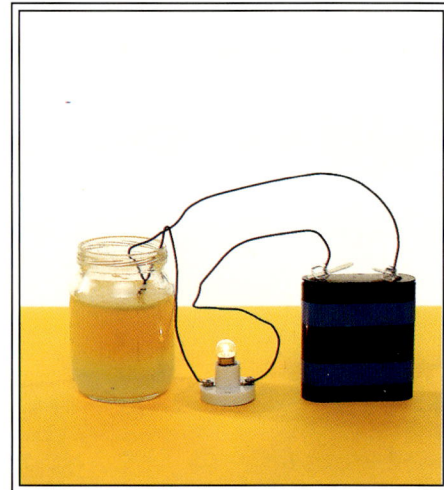

3 The bulb should light to show that electricity is passing through. Carefully sniff the jar from 20cm away. The smell is like swimming pools.

HEAT CHANGES

You will need: *old saucepan, teaspoon, sugar, cooker.*

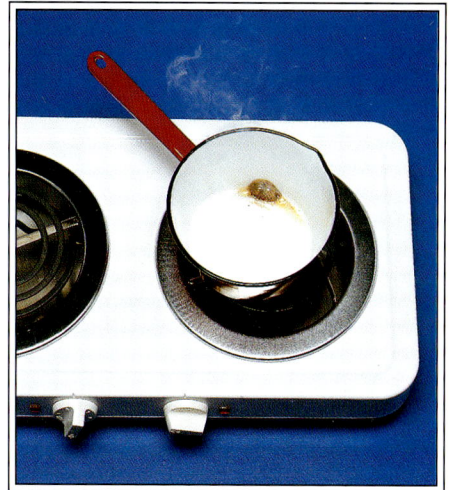

1 Make sure the saucepan is completely dry. Spread one teaspoonful of sugar across the bottom of the pan. Aim for a thin layer a few millimetres thick.

2 Place the pan on a cooker set to low heat. After a few minutes, the sugar starts to melt to give a brown treacly liquid. You may see a few wisps of steam.

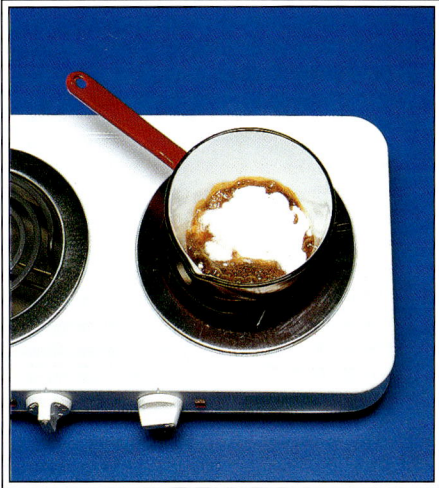

3 The sugar starts to bubble as it breaks down and gives off steam. If you carry on heating, the brown sticky liquid will change to solid black carbon.

MIXING THINGS

You will need: *teaspoon, bicarbonate of soda, glass bowl, spirit vinegar, matches.*

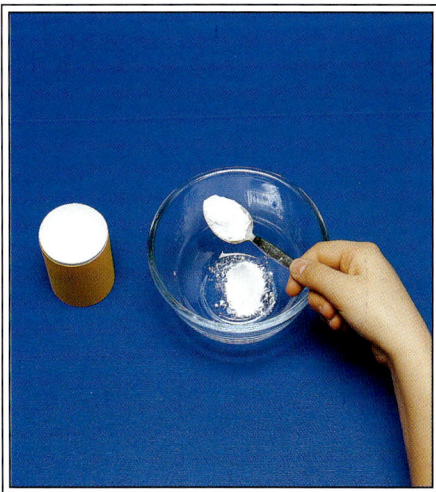

1 Place three heaped spoonfuls of bicarbonate of soda in the bowl. Cooks often add this white powder to vegetables like peas and carrots. It helps to keep their natural colour.

2 Pour vinegar into the bowl. As the liquid mixes with the white powdery bicarbonate of soda, a chemical reaction happens. The mixture bubbles as a gas is given off.

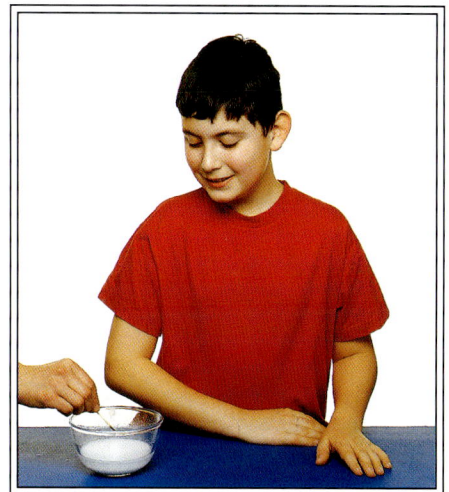

3 Ask an adult to light a match and lower the flame into the bowl. The chemical reaction has made a gas called carbon dioxide. The flame goes out when it meets the gas.

WAIT A SECOND

SOMETIMES we say time hangs heavily on our hands. At other times we say it goes past in a flash. How do we know how much time has actually passed? The easiest way to tell the time is to watch the sun as it rises in the morning and sets in the evening. But people have always wanted to measure time more accurately. This led to the invention of the sundial. The oldest sundials known are Egyptian and more than 5,000 years old.

Today we use clocks and watches to measure time. The first clocks were invented in the 1300s. They had wheels and cogs, weights and pendulums that worked together to turn the hands of the clock. Portable, pocket-size watches were invented in the 1600s, when people discovered how to use springs rather than big weights and pendulums to turn the hands of clocks. Watches became smaller but had to be wound up regularly. In the 1920s the self-winding watch mechanism was invented. Most modern watches are now electronic, not mechanical.

Shadow of time

An ancient Roman sundial is cut in the shape of a shell from a block of marble. Sundials were made in many shapes and sizes. People could judge the time by watching as the shadow cast by the sun moved from one line to another.

Tracking the sun

Before the 1700s, ships' captains relied on quadrants to find out where they were. They used quadrants to estimate the hour of the day, which helped them to know where on the Earth they were. This particular quadrant was designed by the English mathematician, Edmund Gunter, in the early 1600s.

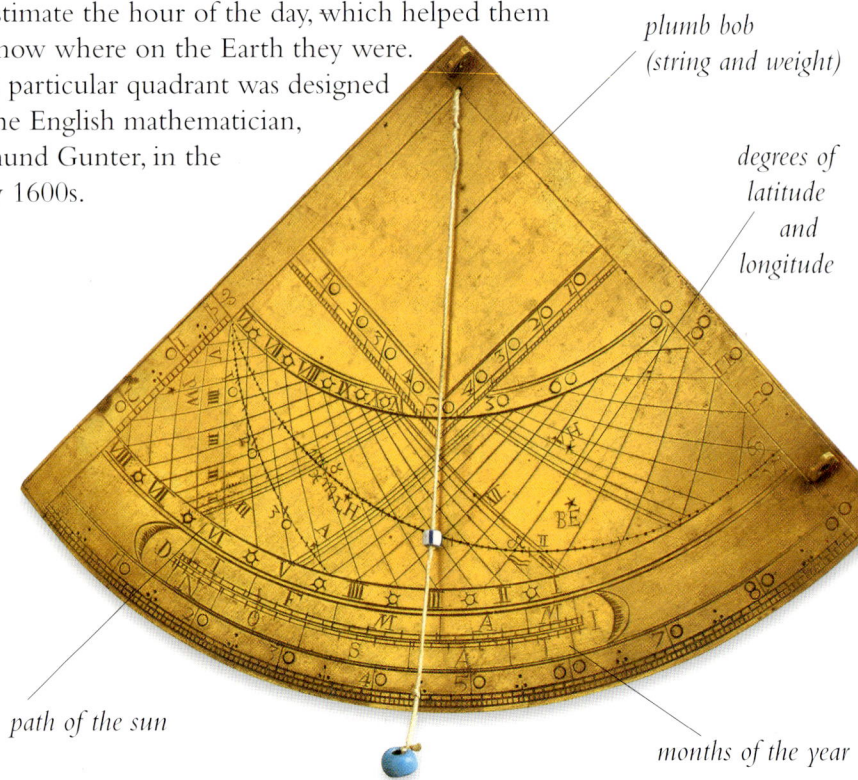

plumb bob (string and weight)

degrees of latitude and longitude

path of the sun

months of the year

The sun and stars

This clock in St Mark's square in Venice dates from the late 1300s. At this time clocks were very large and often built in or near churches because they were too big to fit in homes. Its face is decorated with astrological images of the animals and gods that were used to represent the different seasons and months of the year.

All at sea

Sailors far from land needed to know the time to allow them to work out where they were. They needed accurate clocks to work out the time it had taken to travel a distance. In the 1700s a prize was offered by the British government to invent a marine chronometer (ship's clock) that would keep accurate time on-board ships. John Harrison worked at the problem for 34 years and invented four watches. The last of them won the prize.

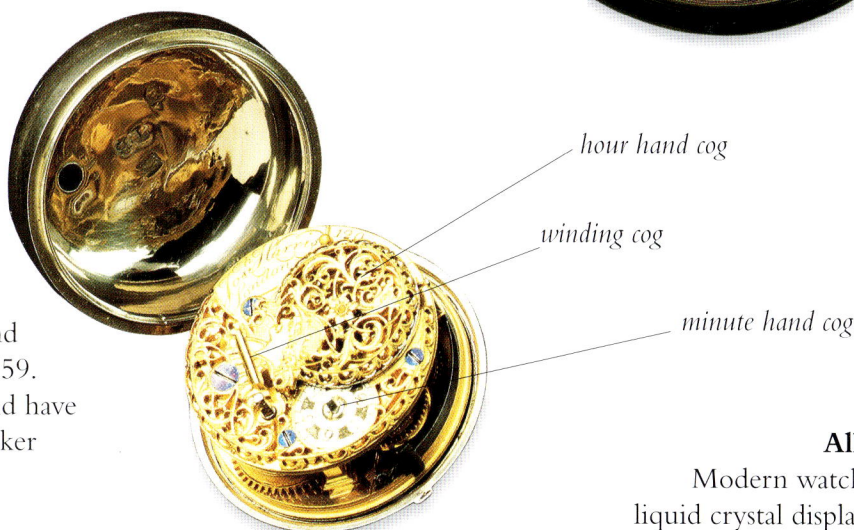

Precious object

A pocket watch was expensive to make and owned only by those with money to spend. A metal case protected the watch from bumps and thumps. This watch was made in 1759. Its many tiny wheels and cogs would have taken months for a skilled watchmaker to make and fit together.

hour hand cog

winding cog

minute hand cog

All in one

Modern watches use a liquid crystal display (LCD) to show the time in digital form. In addition to giving hours and seconds, the watch also displays the day of the week, the month and the year. Other functions can be used by touching the icons at the bottom of the watch face.

Split seconds

Willard Libby, who won the Nobel Prize for Chemistry in 1960, invented the atomic clock. An atomic clock tells the time using the extremely regular changes in the energy inside individual atoms. Clocks such as these can tell the time to within one second over thousands of years.

49

RIVER OF TIME

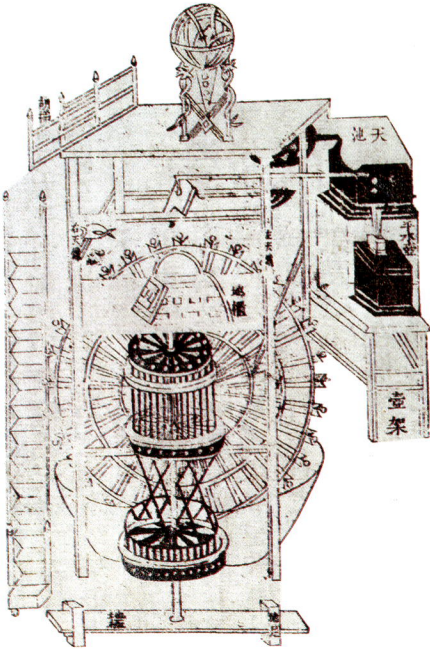

Water timer
This Chinese water clock was built in 1088. Water trickles into tiny buckets fixed to the outside of a large wheel. As each bucket fills up, the wheel clicks round to the next empty bucket. Each bucket empties as it reaches the lowest position. The position of the wheel indicates the time.

THE ancient Egyptians invented water clocks in about 3000BC because the sundials they used could not tell the time at night. Water clocks use water that slowly drips from a bowl and the level of the surface of the remaining water indicates the time. However, a water clock cannot tell the time until you have compared it with another clock. You can make a water clock in the second part of this project.

In 1581, the Italian Galileo Galilei studied how different pendulums swinging back and forth could indicate time. He discovered that the time depends only on the length of the pendulum. It is not affected by the mass of the pendulum, or how far it swings from side to side. You can repeat Galileo's important experiment in the first part of this project. In 1641, Galileo's son Vincenzio Galilei constructed a mechanical clock that used a weighted pendulum to control the speed of hands across a clockface. All grandfather and grandmother clocks work like this. However, pendulums are not always accurate because their speed can vary depending on changes such as heat.

MAKE A PENDULUM

You will need: modelling clay, string, stopwatch.

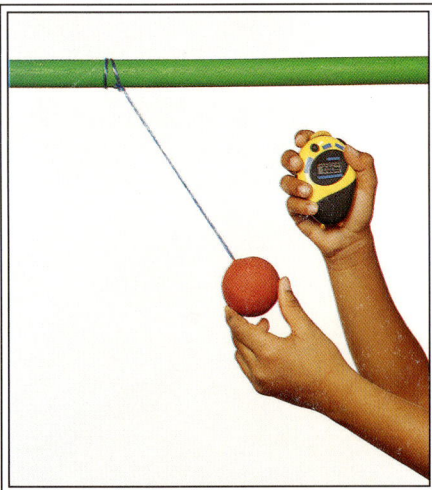

1 Roll some clay to make a ball 4cm across. Use string to hang it 30cm below a support. Pull the ball out to the position shown. Let go and time 10 complete swings.

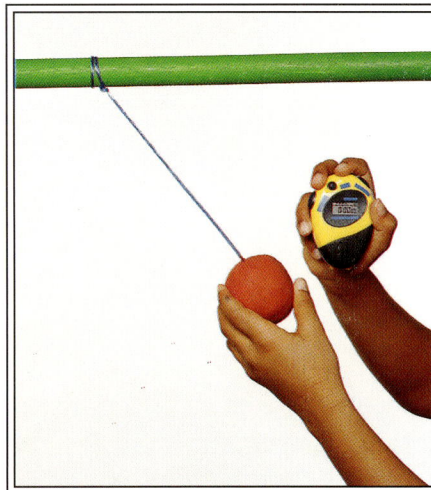

2 Repeat the experiment. This time, use a larger heavier ball with the same bit of string. You will find that the time for ten swings is the same despite the heavier ball.

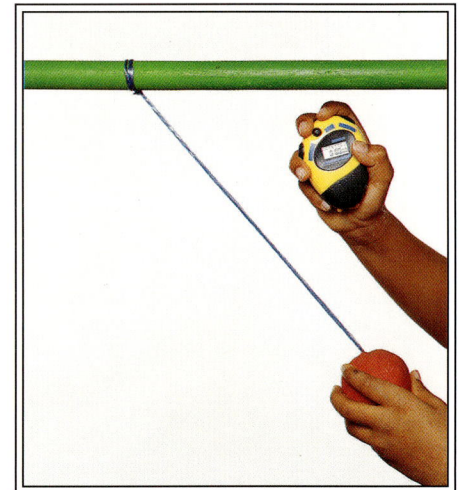

3 Increase the length of your pendulum by hanging the ball from a longer piece of string. You will find that the pendulum swings more slowly than before.

MAKE A
WATER CLOCK

You will need: *bradawl, aluminium pie dish, drinking straw, large plastic tumbler, scissors, water, jug, marker.*

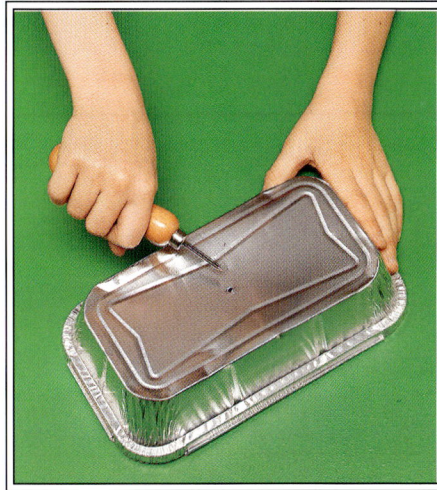

1 Use the bradawl to make a small hole in the bottom of the pie dish. The smaller the hole, the longer your water clock will run.

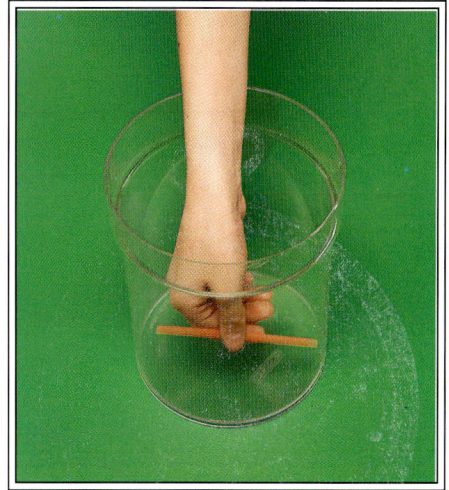

2 Place the drinking straw in the bottom of the plastic tumbler. It will act as a pointer as the water level rises. Cut the straw with a pair of scissors if it is too long.

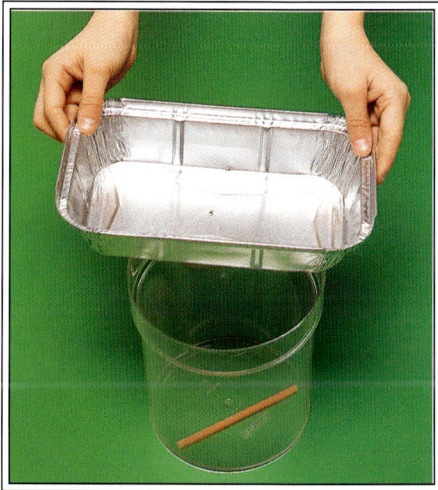

3 Place the pie dish on top of the plastic tumbler. Make sure the hole in the pie dish is over the centre of the tumbler.

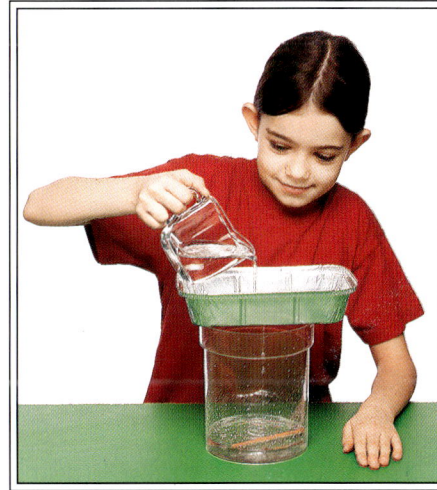

4 Pour water from a jug into the pie dish. Keep adding water until the dish is full. As soon as water starts to fall into the tumbler, note the time on your watch.

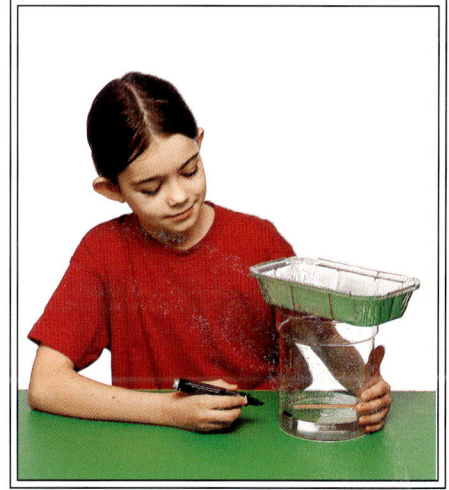

5 After 10 minutes, use the marker to mark the water level on the side of the tumbler. As the water drips into the tumbler, mark the level at 10-minute intervals.

You can use your pie-dish water clock to time your eggs for breakfast.

6 After half an hour you have three marks up the side of the tumbler. Empty out the water, refill the pie dish and you can use your water clock to measure time passing.

CROSSING THE OCEANS

Over the centuries, people have developed ways of crossing the vast seas and oceans of the world. On board ships were pilots, navigators and captains whose job it was to navigate (find directions) across the water and arrive in one particular place. Even from the time of the earliest ship we know of, built for an Egyptian prince's funeral 6,000 years ago, seamen tried to find their way by looking at the position of the stars in the night sky and the sun during the day.

However, it is difficult to calculate exactly where you are from looking at the stars without working out complicated sums using angles and numbers. Over the years a number of instruments such as compasses and octants were invented to help seamen navigate. Maps also helped people to find their way at sea. Early maps did not have very much information. As ever more people travelled to distant places, more detailed maps were drawn of different regions and seas.

Star wheels
The astrolabe, invented by the ancient Greeks, was used for centuries to find directions at sea. The lower disc has a map of the stars and the upper disc has lines showing the heights of stars. This astrolabe dates from the AD1000s.

Looking north
The compass is still one of the most widely used, simple instruments that help people find directions. Chinese and European seamen discovered 700 years ago that a tiny piece of magnetic stone floated on water will always turn towards the Pole Star in the north. Sailors began taking instruments containing pieces of magnetic stone or metal to sea with them. This one dates from the 1300s and the decoration on the top of the compass face shows the direction north.

Charting the seas
Without knowing distances accurately it is very difficult to plan a journey. Making maps of large distances is difficult because the earth is round and maps are flat. It was not until the 1500s that Gerardus Mercator found a way to draw maps like this one of Iceland. It represented the distances on the surface of the earth. Using maps of this kind, travellers could find their way more easily than before.

1761 octant

adjustable screw

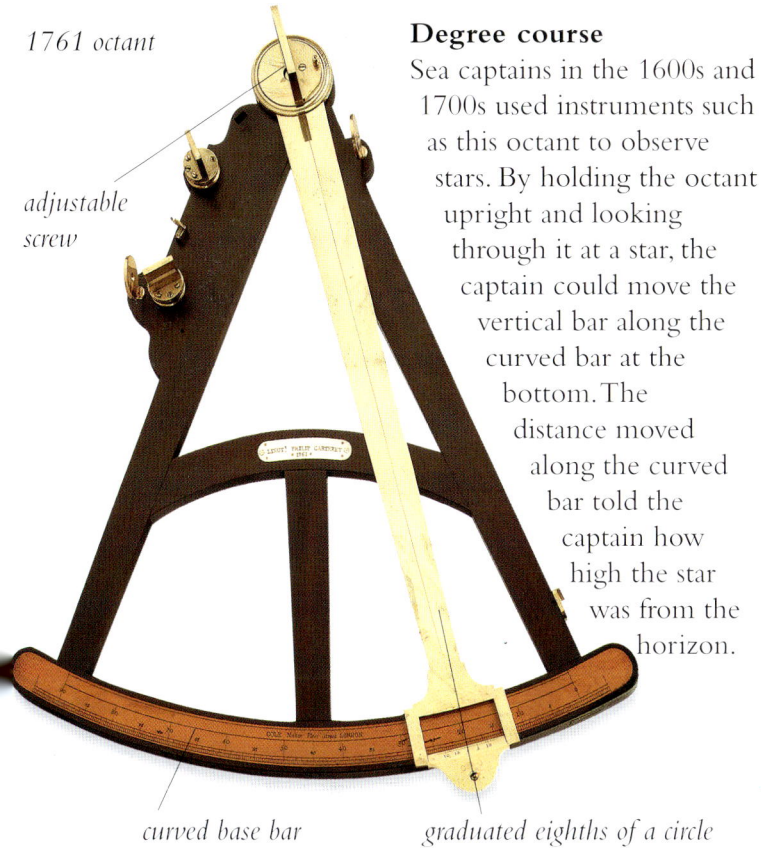

Degree course

Sea captains in the 1600s and 1700s used instruments such as this octant to observe stars. By holding the octant upright and looking through it at a star, the captain could move the vertical bar along the curved bar at the bottom. The distance moved along the curved bar told the captain how high the star was from the horizon.

curved base bar　　　　*graduated eighths of a circle*

Rush for a cuppa

By the 1800s, sea navigation was so highly developed that it was possible to predict how long a ship's journey would take. Very fast ships such as this tea clipper, which carried valuable tea from India, raced one another in the 1860s to see who could make the round trip from India to Britain in the shortest time.

Deep sea hunter

Modern submarines can remain submerged under water for months. Finding directions underwater is even more difficult than on the surface so submarines use a number of ways to navigate. As well as using compasses and maps, they communicate with global positioning satellites (GPS) by radio. The satellites in space send back messages to tell the submarines where they are.

Spectacular sport

Sailing is now a very popular sport and many people all over the world sail boats such as this trimaran for pleasure and in races. Every boat must carry charts, a modern compass and a direction-finding radio before it is considered safe to sail in.

DRIVING AHEAD

THE invention of the wheel was one of the most important technological advances that human beings ever made. It allowed them to travel and transport heavy weights on vehicles pulled by animals such as oxen and horses. Experts believe that knowledge of how to make wheels first developed almost 6,000 years ago in what is now the Middle East. It then spread gradually to people in neighbouring regions. In China, wheels were first made about 3,000 years ago. Some civilizations such as the Aztec and Mayan cultures in America never discovered how to make wheels. Until the invention of the steam engine in the 1800s, wheeled transport could not travel any faster than a horse could gallop. Once steam trains had been invented in the early 1800s, people began to travel faster and faster on land. Early motor cars were very slow because their engines were small and inefficient. However, as engines became bigger, cars travelled faster and faster too.

Flying squad

One immediate effect of inventing the wheel was a revolution in warfare. Racing down on their enemies in a horse-drawn chariot like this one gave the Egyptians a great advantage. War chariots were very light and fast.

FACT BOX

• The world's fastest train is the French *Train à Grande Vitesse*. It travels at speeds up to 300kph during normal journeys, but it is capable of reaching 500kph.

• The diesel engine is named after Rudolf Diesel, who invented it in 1892. Modern diesel engines power cars, trucks and trains.

Pull and push

The first wheels were solid and made out of pieces of wood cut and joined together. Gradually wheels were made lighter and stronger. The spoked wheel on this medieval wagon was the strongest kind of wheel. The spokes absorbed shocks from the wheel as it turned.

Stage by stage

In the 1800s huge numbers of people travelled to the American West when it opened up for settlement. The country was very wild and, until the railroads were built in the 1870s, stagecoaches like this were the only form of public transport. They were very uncomfortable to travel in because they pitched and swayed over rocks and holes in the badly made roads.

First of many

The invention of the steam engine changed the face of transport forever. George Stephenson's *Rocket*, shown here, was built in 1829 and was one of the first steam locomotives. He built it with his son for the Manchester–Liverpool Railway. By the late 1800s, railways stretched all over Europe, North America and much of Asia.

On the cheap

Henry Ford's Model T was the first motor car designed to be built in huge numbers very cheaply. Earlier cars had been hand-made and so were expensive, but Ford designed a system that made it possible to build cheaper cars on an assembly line in a factory. By the time the last Model T came out of the factory in 1927, 15 million had been built since 1908.

Electric engine

Steam railway engines using coal were built in their thousands throughout the 1800s. The first electric locomotives, like this one in Britain, were built in the early 1900s. They were quieter and cleaner than steam engines so they slowly replaced them.

Flash motor

Some of the earliest cars were built by Karl Benz in the late 1800s. He founded a factory that expanded to become the company that built this modern car. This Mercedes–Benz S430L can travel at a top speed of 240 kph. It is equipped with modern safety features such as airbags and uses tiny computers that control the car's stability and braking.

FLYING HIGH

BIRDS and insects fly by using their wings to lift off the ground and support their weight on currents of air. Although humans have never had wings, they have always wanted to fly like birds. Scientists and inventors looked for ways to make artificial wings for hundreds of years.

Kites were invented in China 2,000 years ago and may have been used for military purposes. In the 1780s, the Montgolfier brothers flew in balloons over France. Balloons, however, proved too difficult to steer to be practical. Powered flight has only been possible in the past hundred years. The Wright brothers flew their first aeroplane in 1903, in the USA, and showed that it is possible to control the movement of an aircraft. Like the invention of the wheel, the discovery of flight changed warfare. Air power was used in war only 11 years after the Wright brothers' first flight. Commercial air travel became more and more popular from the 1960s onward.

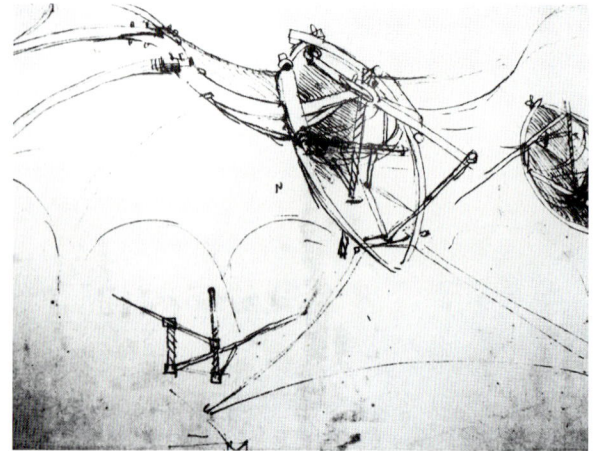

Bird man
The Italian artist and inventor Leonardo da Vinci drew designs for flying machines in the early 1500s. This drawing shows wings that could be strapped to the arms to allow the wearer to fly. However, they were never built.

Keep going
This is one of the Wright brothers' first aircraft, the first successful flying machine. One engine attached to the frame turned propellers and created enough power to keep the aircraft moving forward. This provided the essential lift from air rushing past under and over the wings to keep it airborne.

Blades of power
A jet turbine takes in air through the front blades. As the blades turn faster they compress the air which is ignited. The second blades are moved by the burning air which then turns the compressor. This drives the aircraft on.

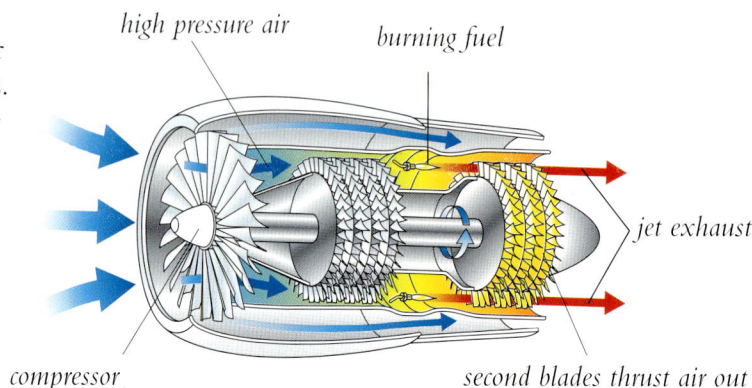

high pressure air

burning fuel

jet exhaust

compressor

second blades thrust air out

Whirly bird
The man sitting at the controls of this early helicopter is the Russian-born Igor Sikorsky. After 1917, he went to live in the USA and worked as an aeroplane engineer. By 1940, he had developed the first successful vertical take-off helicopter and flew several of the early machines he built.

Flying boat

The largest commercial aircraft built between World War I and World War II were flying boats of the kind shown here. Because there were few long runways built on land, large planes often took off from, and landed on, water. This six-engined plane flew on routes between Italy and South America.

Two in one

The Harrier jump-jet is a unique type of aircraft. It can land and take off vertically like a helicopter, but it flies like a jet. The aircraft has movable jet thrusters that are vertical when landing and taking off but horizontal when in flight. This type of aircraft is mainly used for military purposes.

Wide blue yonder

The Space Shuttle is the ultimate aircraft. It takes off vertically attached to rocket boosters, to reach orbit around the Earth. When it returns from orbit, the Shuttle glides through the atmosphere and lands just like any jet plane.

Jetsetter

The de Havilland *Comet* shown here was the first jet aircraft to go into regular passenger service. It began flying in 1952 and halved the time for long journeys such as that between London and South Africa. By 1958, regular jet flights between Britain and the USA meant transatlantic jet travel had come to stay.

NUMBER CRUNCHERS

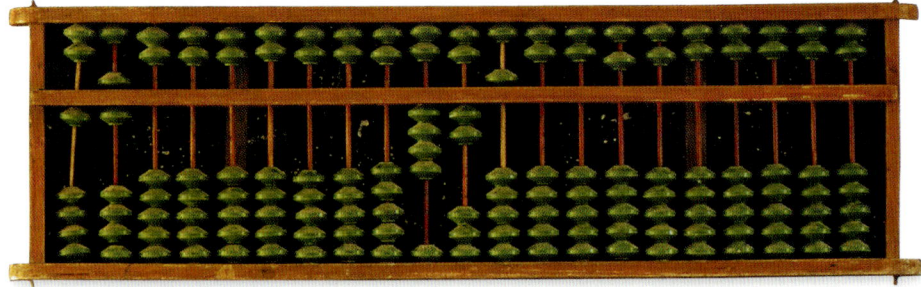

It is not certain exactly when people first invented numbers. We do know, however, that numbers were in use by the time the first civilizations grew up, 6,000 years ago. In these early societies, numbers allowed people to count possessions when trading and to note the days of the week and months of the year. The Greek inventor Hero of Alexandria designed a counting machine 2,000 years ago and, in the early 1500s, Leonardo da Vinci also designed one. In 1835 Charles Babbage invented a mechanical calculator called the difference engine. A mechanical calculator was later used to break codes (secret communications) during World War II. These machines were the first computers. Afterwards, ever larger electronic computers were built, and in the 1980s small personal computers (PCs) appeared in offices and at home.

Counter culture

People have been using this kind of counting device for thousands of years. It is known in China as a *suan pan* and as an abacus in English. Beads are arranged on vertical, parallel strings. Each string represents different kinds of number. For example, on the extreme left are 1s, next left 10s. By sliding the beads up and down, a person can quickly perform complicated arithmetic.

Brass and steel

The difference engine is a complicated arrangement of metal cogs and ratchets designed to count numbers mechanically. It was invented by Charles Babbage in 1835 but he never succeeded in finishing it. Building such a machine out of solid metal parts without any electrical circuits is extremely difficult.

Code breaker

Colossus was the name given to this computer built at Bletchley in Britain during World War II. It was used to break codes used by German commanders who sent orders by radio. The orders were sent as constantly changing groups of letters that only made sense to those who knew the key. *Colossus* performed the millions of calculations necessary to read the code even though the British did not have the key.

Micro-maze

Silicon chips allow modern computers to perform millions of calculations in a second. Before chips were invented, enormous boxes were needed to hold all the wires required to calculate electronically. Then miniaturization was invented. This made it possible to put many tiny circuits on to one piece of silicon.

Carry on computing

A small computer can be carried and used anywhere. Batteries inside supply power for the hardware. Portable computers are often called laptops because they are small and light enough to place on a sitting person's lap.

A boring box

This very uninteresting looking box is in fact one of the world's fastest computers. There is little to look at on the outside because everything interesting is inside, where thousands of chips can calculate trillions of numbers every second.

Out into space

To operate in space without human help, spacecraft such as the *Voyager* probe are equipped with computers that control them. Without small computers, spacecraft would never be able to leave Earth. They would need to carry machines to control them so large that the spacecraft would weigh far too much to leave the earth's surface.

THROUGH THE LOGIC GATE

INFORMATION flowing inside a computer is called data. It is in the form of electrical pulses. Data changes as it passes through part of the computer called the central processing unit (CPU). The CPU has thousands of separate high-speed switches called logic gates. These logic gates are microscopic transistors cut into a silicon chip. They can flick on and off up to 300 million times a second. Data flows into the input side of each gate. It only flows out again if the gate is switched on. The computer program sets up how the gates switch on and off and so controls the data flow through the computer.

There are three main types of gates, called AND, NOT, and OR gates. Working together, they act as counters or memory circuits to store data. Logic gates are also used to control things like washing machines. In this project, you can make a model AND gate to show how the output depends on the settings of the two input connections.

AND gate		
Input A	Input B	Output C
OFF	OFF	OFF
OFF	ON	OFF
OFF	ON	OFF
ON	ON	ON

OR gate		
Input A	Input B	Output C
OFF	OFF	OFF
OFF	ON	ON
ON	OFF	ON
ON	ON	ON

On or off?
AND and OR gates both have two inputs (A and B) and one output connection (C). The tables show how the ON/OFF states of the inputs affect the ON/OFF state of the output. These tables are called truth tables.

MAKE A LOGIC GATE

You will need: felt-tipped pen, ruler, stiff card in 3 colours, scissors, stapler, pencil, red and green sticky circles.

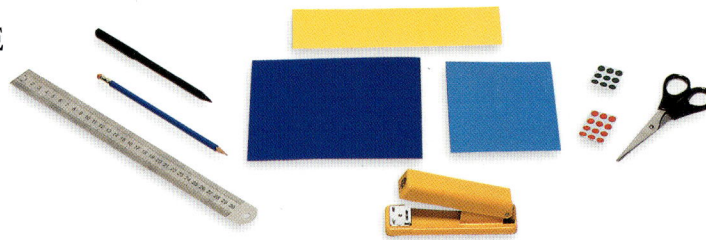

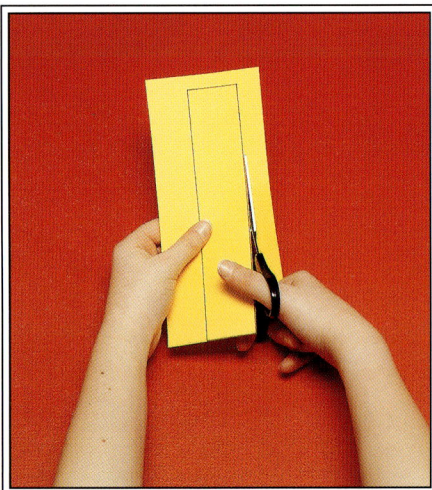

1 Mark and cut out three pieces of card. Referring to the colours shown here, the sizes are: dark blue 15 x 10cm, light blue 10 x 7cm and yellow 4 x 20cm.

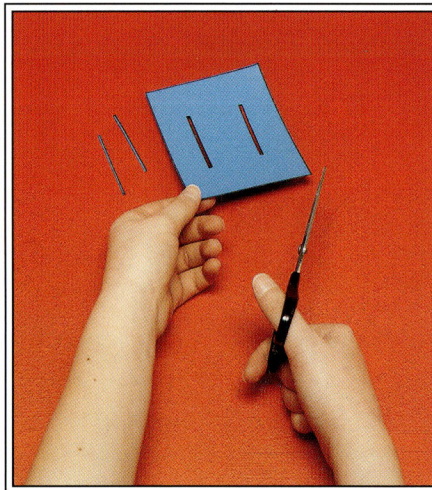

2 On the 10 x 7cm card, draw two slots that are slightly more than 4cm wide and 4cm apart. Cut each slot so that it is about 2 – 3mm wide.

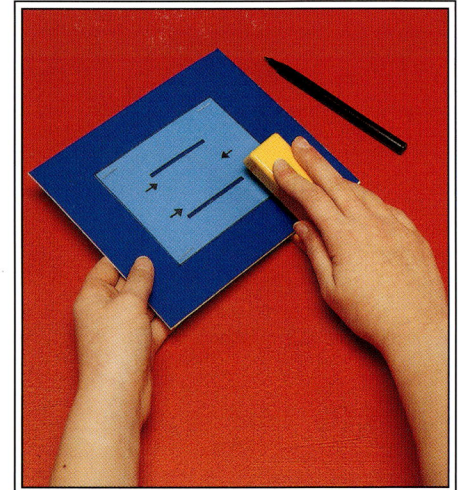

3 Place the card with slots in the centre of the dark blue card. Staple them together with one staple at each corner of the top card. Draw the three arrows as shown.

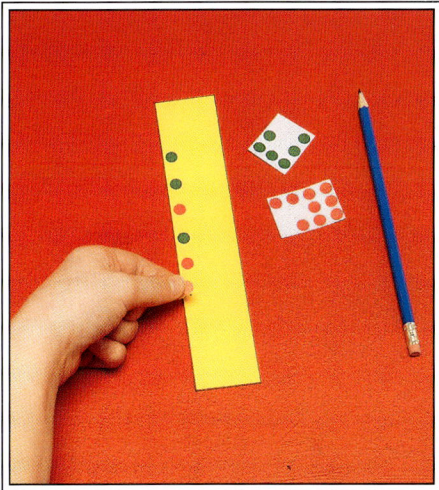

4 At 2cm intervals, stick coloured circles in the order shown on to the left side of the long card strip. This is the input side.

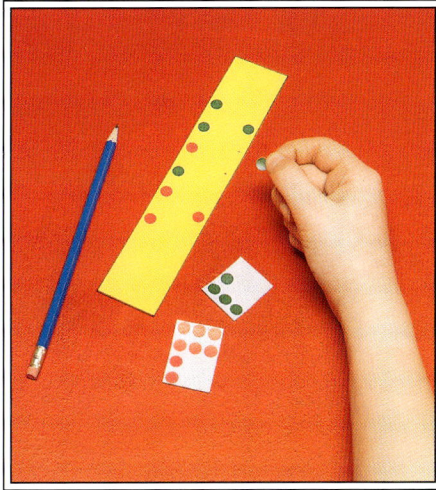

5 Add coloured stickers to the right (output side) at 4cm intervals in this order: green, red, red, red. Notice that each sticker is midway between the two on the left.

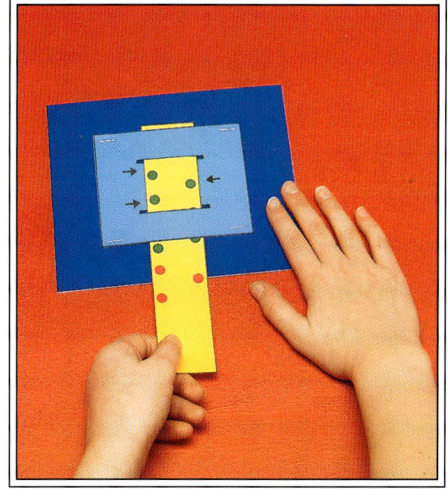

6 Push the strip between the two stapled cards and feed it through the lower slot. Keep pushing the strip and feed it through the top slot and out between the stapled cards.

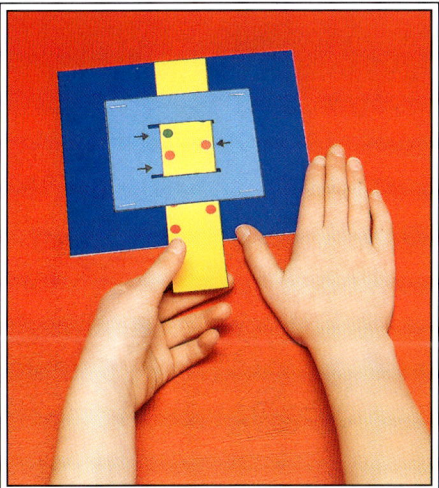

7 Move the strip until there is a green dot at the top of the input side. There should be a green dot on the output side, showing that both inputs must be ON for the output to be ON.

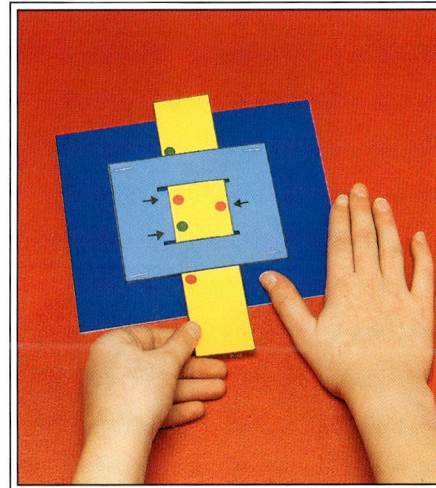

8 When the input shows red at the top with a green dot below, then a green dot appears on the output side. Your model is showing that the output is OFF when only one input is ON.

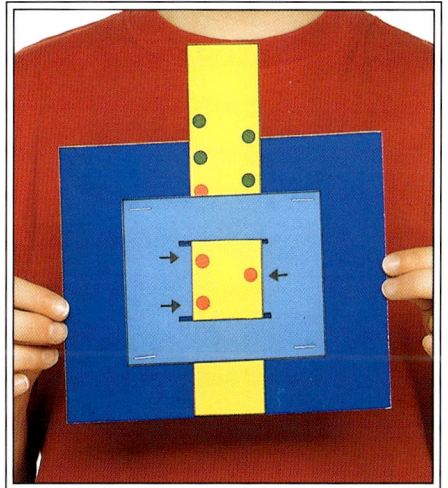

9 Here is your completed model AND gate. Now make a similar model with the stickers in the right places to show how an OR gate works. You will find that AND gates and OR gates are very different.

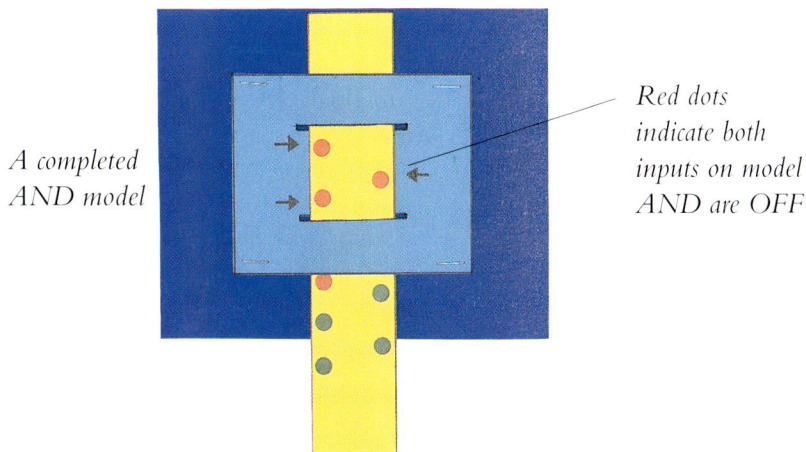

A completed AND model

Red dots indicate both inputs on model AND are OFF

10 When both inputs on your model AND gate show red, then a red dot appears opposite the output. As you might expect, the output of an AND gate is OFF when both inputs are OFF.

THINGS TO COME

THE pace of invention has increased dramatically since the 1800s and there is no sign of it slowing down. Almost every week new inventions are announced. A recent invention for replanting trees by dropping saplings from the air could make forests grow again in many parts of the earth. Computerized map systems have been developed that make it impossible to get lost when travelling.

Many new inventions are things we hardly notice, such as the material Velcro which holds surfaces together and is used in place of buttons and zips on clothes. Some inventions are useful only in special situations. Kevlar is a recently invented, bullet-proof material that is very valuable for soldiers and policemen but little used in everyday life. Understanding of the genetic structures of living bodies is increasing all the time. In the future people may be able to choose what colour their baby's hair will be! One thing is certain. Whatever happens, people will not stop inventing.

Electronic circuits
Semiconductors are essential for making many of the electronic devices that we use every day, from pocket calculators to personal computers. Semiconductors are used to make electricity flow through tiny circuits in complex patterns that control how machines work.

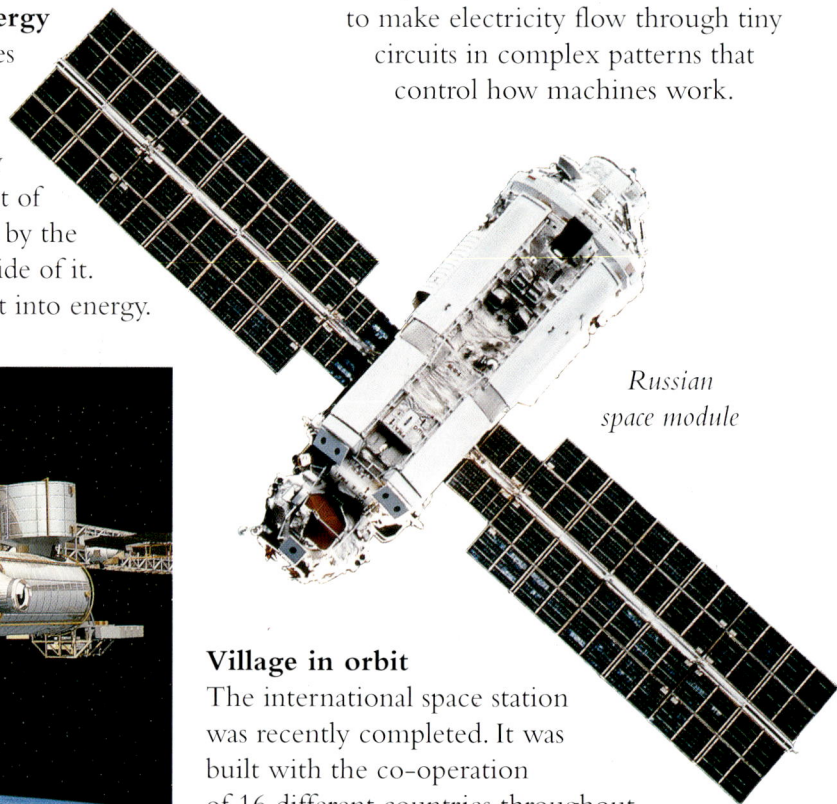

Solar energy
People are trying increasingly to find new sources of energy because the old ones, such as coal and gas, will be used up in the future. Solar energy (the heat and light of the Sun) is one new energy source. This Russian space module, part of the international space station (ISS), is powered by the solar energy panels that fan out on either side of it. The panels convert heat and light into energy.

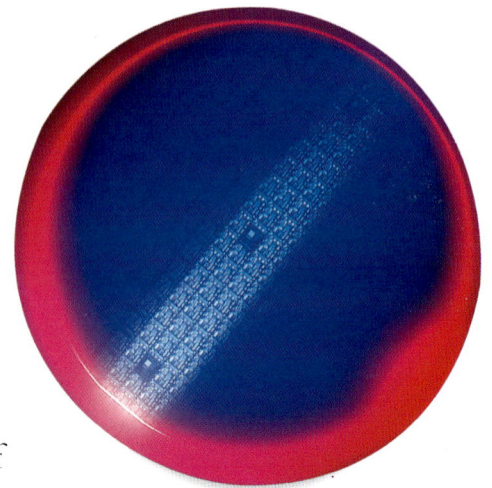

Russian space module

Village in orbit
The international space station was recently completed. It was built with the co-operation of 16 different countries throughout the world. They hope that having this permanent space station in orbit will allow scientists to make discoveries in space that will advance medicine, science and engineering.

Touchy-feely

Virtual reality is an invention that allows users wearing a headset and gloves to see and feel scenes which exist only on computer. Looking and touching in this way can be a very helpful way of training people to use machines. For example, pilots can be trained to fly a new aircraft without actually going into the air.

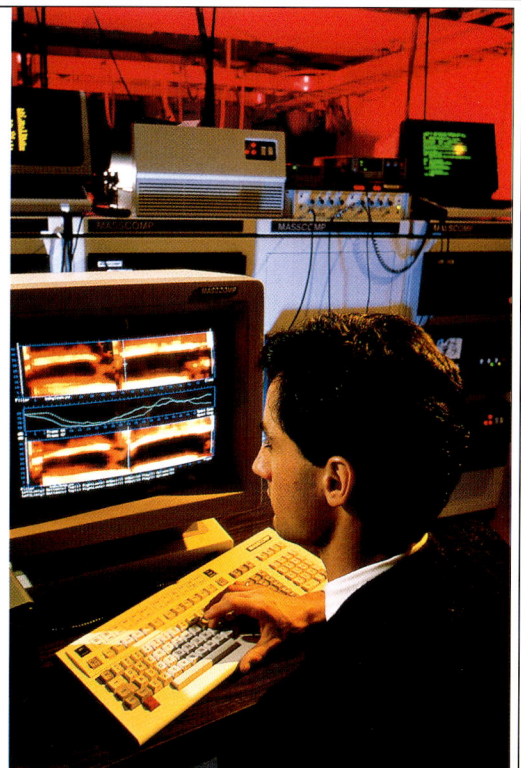

Talk to me

A scientist is looking at a graph that shows the word "baby" on a computer screen. It is part of research into how computers can reply to human voices. If people could talk to computers, using them would be easier.

Safe energy

The biggest problem with energy produced using nuclear fuel is the danger of radiation that can kill people. Some scientists recently believed that they had found a way to generate energy using the cold-fusion process shown here. The process creates energy by nuclear fusion without making radioactivity. It is uncertain whether this process can be used on a large scale or even repeated easily.

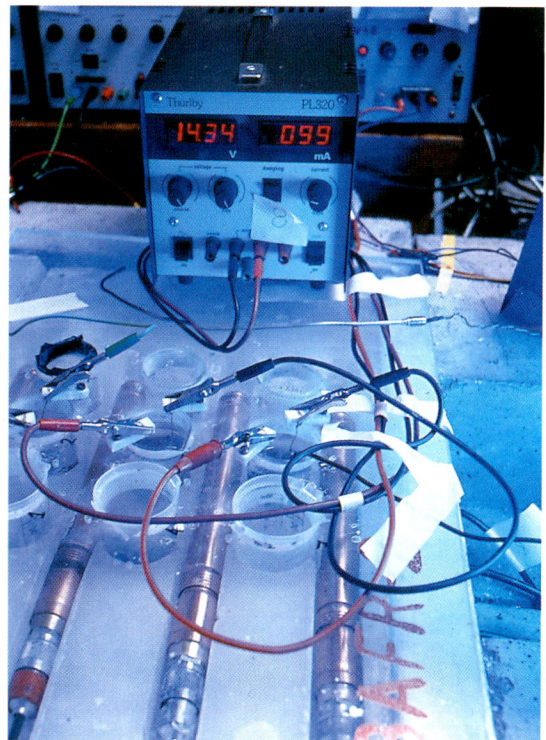

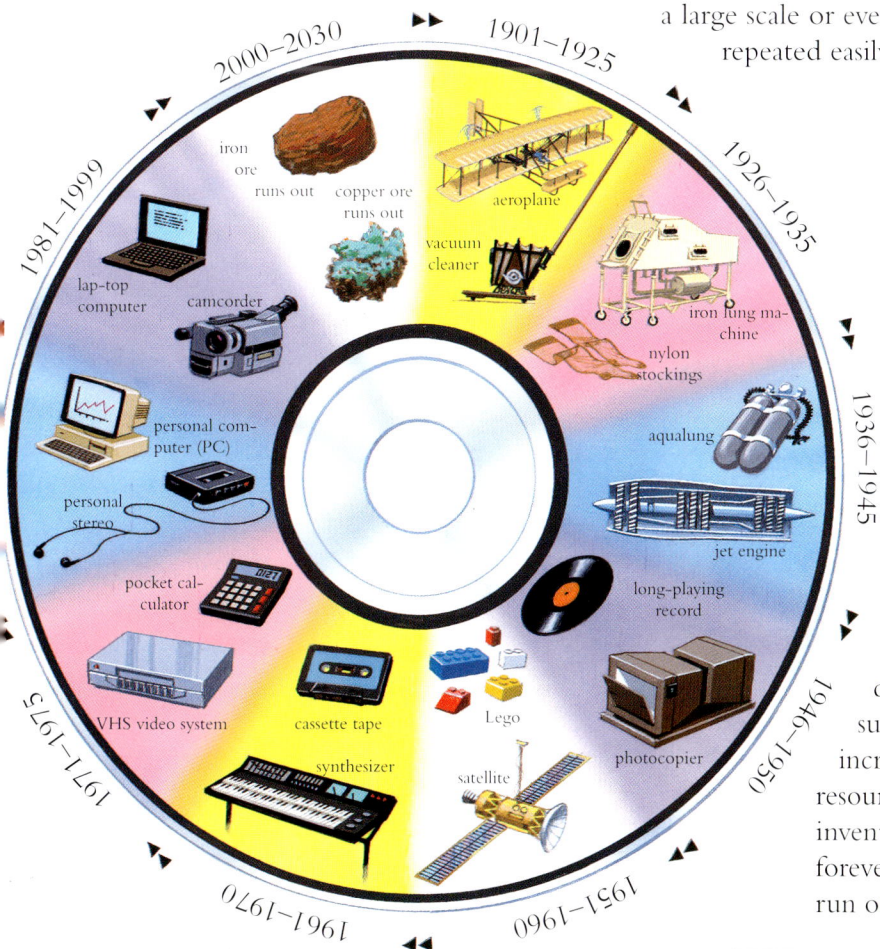

2000–2030
1901–1925
1981–1999
1926–1935
1936–1945
1971–1975
1961–1970
1951–1960
1946–1950

iron ore runs out
copper ore runs out
aeroplane
vacuum cleaner
iron lung machine
nylon stockings
aqualung
jet engine
long-playing record
photocopier
satellite
Lego
synthesizer
cassette tape
VHS video system
pocket calculator
personal stereo
personal computer (PC)
lap-top computer
camcorder

Still turning

Some of the many inventions since 1900 are shown inside the circle of this CD (compact disc). In the last 40 years electronic inventions, such as video and CD technology, have been used increasingly in homes everywhere. However, the resources on which people rely to make new inventions, such as copper and iron, will not last forever. In particular, copper ore will start to run out in 25 years' time.

MACHINES

WHAT IS A MACHINE?

Thousands of different devices can be called machines, from calculators and televisions to trucks and aircraft. Scissors and staplers are very simple machines, while computers and cars are complicated. All machines have one thing in common – they help us do jobs and so make our lives easier.

Think about what you did yesterday. Make a list of every machine you can remember that you used or saw, from when you woke up to when you went back to bed. Many things that we take for granted, such as opening a tin can, cutting paper or tightening a screw, can only be done with a machine. Other jobs, such as washing clothes, used to be done by hand but nowadays are usually done by machine. Machines are being improved – and new ones invented – all the time. We may find that tasks that take a long time today become much easier and faster to do in the future.

screwdriver

pliers

scissors

hammer

Allen keys

Simple machines

Tools such as these are simple machines that are useful to have at home. They each do a task that would be much more difficult without them. Can you think of a job for each tool?

Useful screws

The parts of this model helicopter are fixed together with screws. The screws are machines because they do the job of holding the helicopter parts in place.

Domestic machines

A microwave oven is one of the many machines that people use at home to make preparing and cooking food quicker and simpler. Other domestic machines include vacuum cleaners and washing machines.

Using tools

This girl uses a spanner to tighten the nuts on her model helicopter. A spanner is a simple tool that is used to tighten up, or undo, nuts. Using the spanner is more efficient than if the girl used her fingers alone, because the spanner can make joints much tighter and more secure.

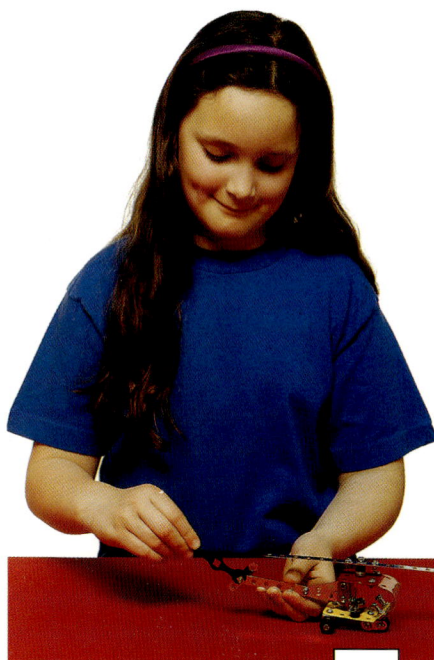

FACT BOX

• Leonardo da Vinci (1452–1519) was an Italian artist and inventor. He drew plans for machines, such as tanks and aircraft, that were hundreds of years ahead of their time.

• Greek scientist Hero of Alexandria lived in the 1st century AD. He invented a steam engine, a slot machine and a screw press.

Old farm machines

People use many different machines to help them farm the land in this picture, which was painted in about 1400. Some of the first machines ever invented were used by farmers. At the bottom of the picture is a plough, and halfway up on the right-hand side is a water-wheel. At the top, by a church, is a machine called a shaduf, which was used to raise water from a deep well. Next to the shaduf is a machine that was used for sowing seed.

Calculating machine

Unlike most of the other machines shown here, a computer does not help lift, move or cut things. Instead it makes life easier by remembering information and doing calculations. Computers help us to work faster and more accurately. They can do amazing work – such as controlling the flight path of a spacecraft.

Construction machines

Diggers and cranes are used on a construction (building) site. These huge machines are clearing the site of rubble before the buildings are restored. Construction machines have powerful engines for moving and lifting heavy loads, such as soil, rocks, steel and concrete.

Travel by machine

To travel from place to place you need a machine to get you there. The space shuttle is a machine that transports people into space. Its powerful rocket engines launch it through Earth's atmosphere. Other transport machines, such as cars and trains, also have engines. Their engines are much less powerful than those on a spacecraft.

Chopping machine

A hand axe is used to chop large logs into smaller pieces. When the woman brings the axe down, the sharp blade slices into the wood, forcing it to split apart. The axe is a simple machine, but it is very effective. It does a job that is impossible to do by hand.

POWERFUL LEVERS

Six simple machines that were invented thousands of years ago are still the basic elements of all machinery. These machines are the lever, the wheel and axle, the inclined plane or ramp, the wedge, the screw and the pulley. The simplest, and probably the oldest, is the lever. A lever is a bar or rod that tilts on an object called a pivot. You only need a small push down on one end to raise a large weight on the end nearer to the pivot. Any rod or stick can act as a lever, helping to move heavy objects or prise things apart. The lever makes the power of the push into a much larger push. This is known as mechanical advantage.

Did you know that some parts of your body are levers? Every time you brush your hair or get up from a chair, the bones in your arms and legs act as levers, helping you to lift your limbs.

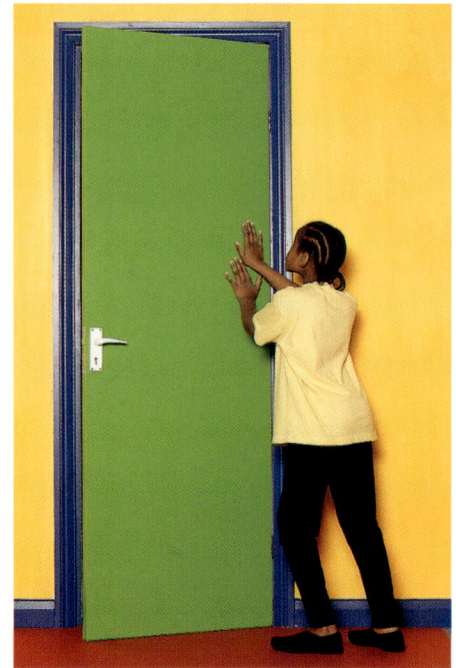

How a lever works
A lever tilts on a pivot, which is nearer to the end of the lever with the load on it. The effort, or force, is the push you make on the long end of the lever to lift the weight of the load.

effort

pivot

load

Using a simple lever
A spoon can be a lever. The girl is using the spoon as a simple lever to lift the lid off a tin of paint. The lever arm pivots on the lip of the tin. As the girl pushes down on the long end, the shorter end wedged under the lid lifts it up with great force, making the stiff lid move.

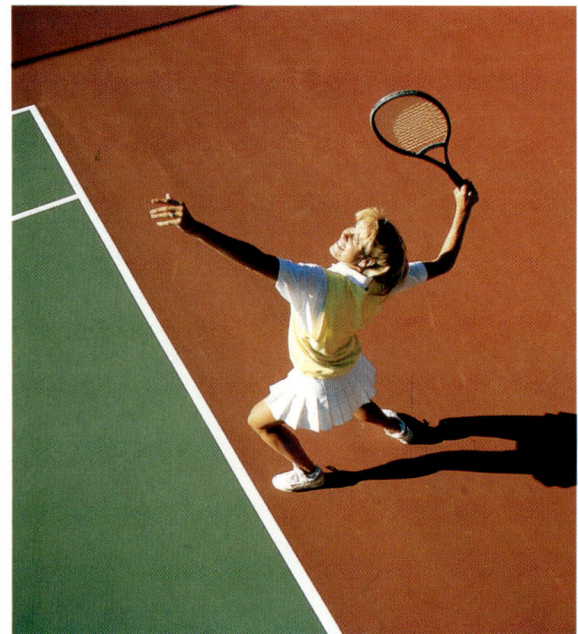

Shut the door
Closing a door near the hinge is hard work. It is easier to press on the handle because the door is a lever. Its pivot is made by the hinges. The door turns your small push on the handle into a bigger push.

Levers in the body
A tennis player uses muscle-powered levers in her shoulders and elbows to serve the ball at high speed. Small movements of the muscles cause large movements of the racket, which gives the racket the speed for a fast serve.

LEVERS AND LIFTING

1 A ruler can be used as a lever to lift a book. With the pivot (the box) near the book, only a small effort is needed to lift the book up. The lever makes the push larger.

2 When the pivot is moved to the middle of the lever, the effort needed to lift the book up is equal to the book's weight. The effort and the load are the same.

3 When the pivot is near where the boy is pressing, more effort is needed to lift the book. The force of the push needed to lift the book is now larger than the book's weight.

Raising water

In Middle Eastern countries, farmers use a machine called a shaduf to lift water to irrigate their crops. The arm of a shaduf is a lever with a bucket on one end and a weight on the other, pivoted on the top of a wooden frame. The shaduf operator pulls the empty bucket down into the water using a rope. The weight at the other end acts as the effort, lifting the bucket of water (the load). The shaduf is an ancient machine, used by farmers for thousands of years.

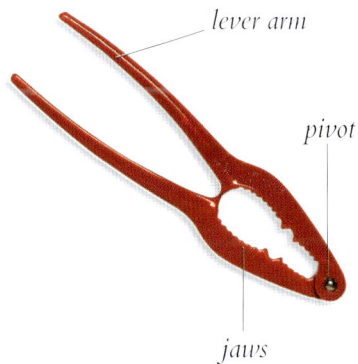

lever arm

pivot

jaws

The strong crushing action of the nutcracker's jaws is produced by pressing the two lever arms together.

Cracking a nut

A pair of nutcrackers, like a pair of scissors or a pair of pliers, has two lever arms joined at a pivot. Pressing the ends of the nutcracker arms together squashes the nut in its jaws. The levers make the effort you use about four times bigger, allowing you to break the nut quite easily. Putting the pivot at the end of the levers rather than towards the centre (as in a pair of scissors) means that the arms of the cracker can be shorter but still create a force just as big.

BALANCING LEVERS

Levers are used for lifting, cutting and squashing. A lever on a central pivot can also be used as a balance. The lever balances if the effect of the force (push) on one side of the pivot is the same as the effect of the force on the other. A see-saw is one sort of balancing lever. It is a plank balanced on a central post or pivot. Someone small and light can balance a much bigger person if they sit in the right position on a see-saw.

Outside the playground, balancing levers have other important uses. By using a lever to balance one force with another, the size of one force can be compared to the size of another. This is how a weighing machine called a balance scale works. It measures the mass (weight) of an object by comparing it with standard weights such as grams and kilograms.

Weighing up
Balance scales like this one were once used for weighing things in shops or in the kitchen. To make the lever arm balance, the weights on the left must equal the weight in the pan.

Using a balance scale
An object, such as a pile of strawberries, is put in a pan resting on one end of the lever arm. Weights are added to the other end of the arm until the arm balances. Then the individual weights are added up to find the weight of the object. We call the result 'weight' because we measure the force needed to balance the weight of the object. In fact, a balance scale measures kilograms.

Balanced crossing gates
A level-crossing gate is actually a balanced lever. The pivot is at the side of the road, with the gate to one side and a heavy counterweight on the other side to balance it. This means that only a small effort is needed from electric motors to move the lever up or down. The gates are operated automatically by electronics linked to the railway's signalling system.

Two children of equal weight, the same distance from the pivot, make the see-saw balance.

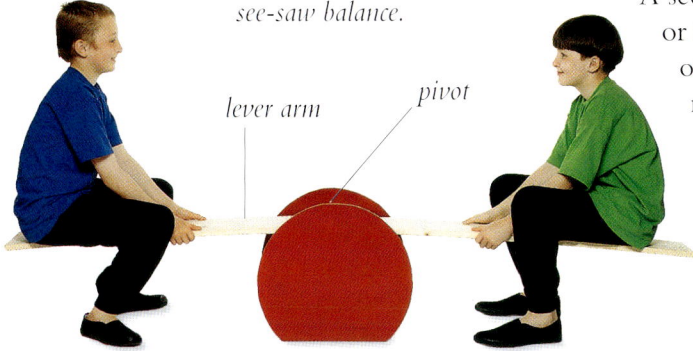

lever arm   pivot

Balancing a see-saw

A see-saw shows the effect of moving a weight nearer or farther from the pivot of a lever arm. Two children of equal weight, the same distance from the pivot, make a see-saw balance. If another child is added to one end, the arm overbalances to that side. By moving the single child farther from the pivot, or the pair closer to it, the arm balances again.

By adding another child to one side, that side overbalances. The pair's greater weight easily lifts the lighter boy.

By moving the pair nearer the pivot, their weight can be balanced by the lighter boy moving farther away.

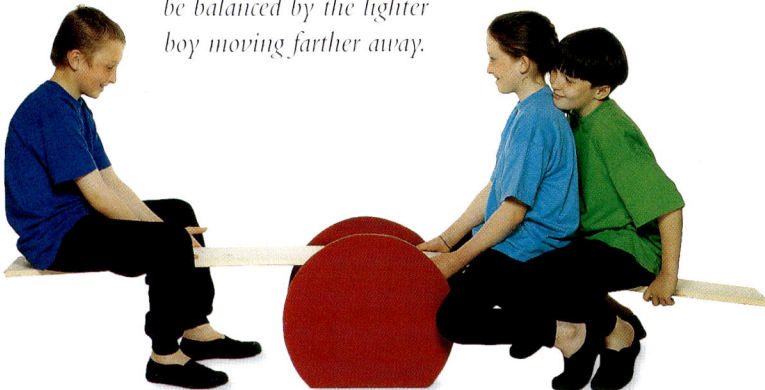

Investigating balance

Make a ruler balance on a tube. Now put different-sized piles of coins at different positions on each end so that they balance. For example, you can make one coin balance two coins if the single coin is twice as far from the pivot as the other coins.

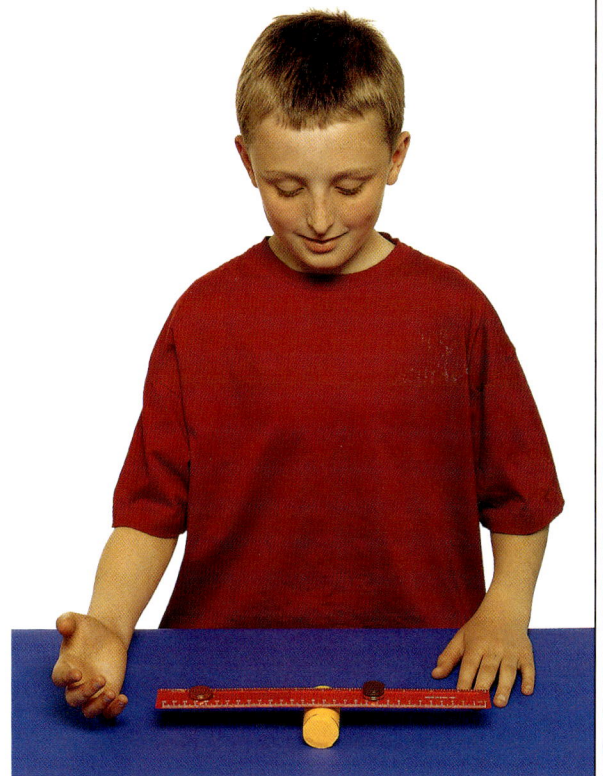

71

ALL KINDS OF LEVERS

Levers are very common machines. Look around you and see how many levers you can spot – don't forget the levers in your own body! Each of the machines shown here has a diagram to show you where the pivot, effort and load are, to help you to see how the lever is working.

Levers are divided into three different basic kinds, or classes. The most common type is a first-class lever, where the pivot is always between the load and the effort, as with a see-saw, a pair of pliers or a spade. In second-class levers, the load is between the pivot and the effort. Nutcrackers and wheelbarrows are examples of these. In a third-class lever, the effort is between the pivot and the load, as with hammers, tweezers and fishing rods.

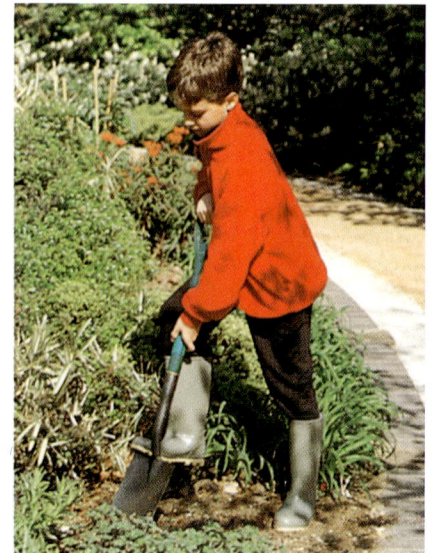

Spade work

A spade is a first-class lever for lifting and turning soil. A sharp blade makes it easy to push the spade into the soil. Pressing down on the handle is the effort, the pivot is the surface of the soil behind the blade and the load is the soil in front of it. Pushing the handle down levers the soil up.

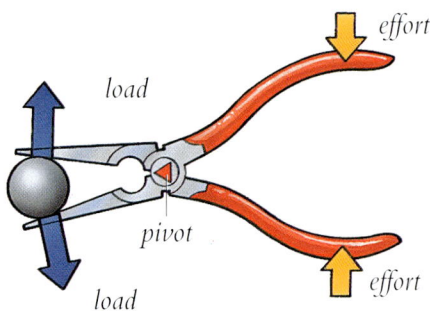

In a pair of pliers, the effort is pressing down on handles. The load is the resistance that an object has to being crushed in the jaws of the pliers.

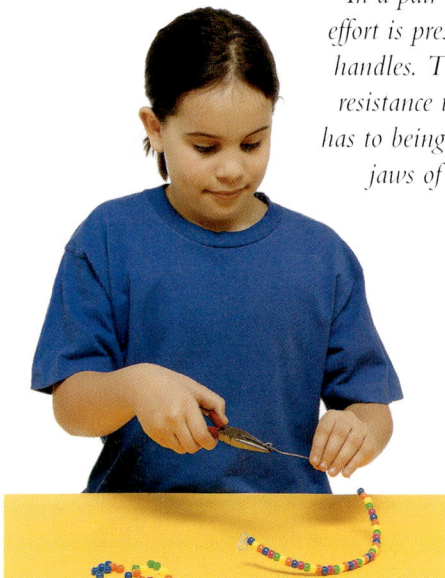

Lifting the handles of a wheelbarrow lifts a heavy load nearer the pivot, or wheel.

Second-class levers

A wheelbarrow does not look like a lever, but it is one. The lever arm goes from the end of the handle to the centre of the wheel, which is the pivot. A small effort pulling up on the handles lifts the load in the barrow.

First-class levers

A pair of pliers has two lever arms linked at the pivot by a hinge. They are first-class levers because the pivot is between the load and the effort. The handles are on one side of the pivot and the jaws are on the other.

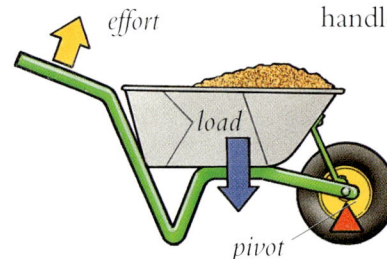

72

A hammer acts as a lever when you use your wrist as a pivot. Your fingers make the effort to lift the hammer's head.

Third-class levers

A hammer may not look like a lever, but it is. The handle joins with your hand to make the lever arm, with your wrist as the pivot. Your fingers supply the effort to make the hammer head move down. The load is the weight of the hammer head. The small movement of your arm makes a large movement in the hammer head to drive the nail into the wood.

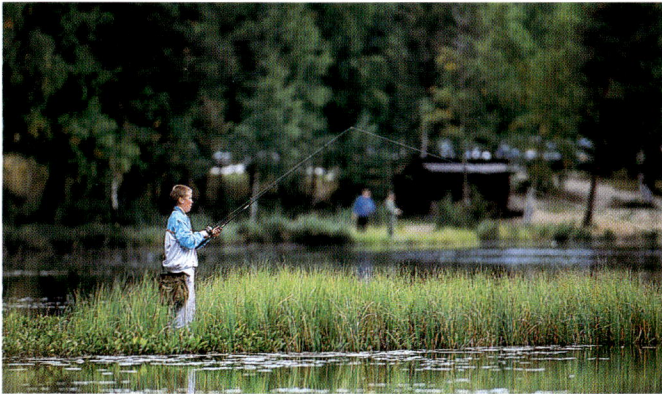

Gone fishing

A fishing rod is a third-class lever, similar to the hammer above. The pivot is at the fisherman's wrist. The effort is made by his hand, and the load is the weight of the rod and the fish on the line. An effort much greater than the load is needed to lift the rod. The advantage of the rod is that a small movement of the fisherman's arm makes a large movement at the end of the rod. So a flick of the wrist casts the line which floats far across the water.

FACT BOX

• The longer a lever arm, the greater the force. Using a lever (it would have to be a strong lever) 10m long, with a pivot 10cm from the end, you could lift an elephant with one finger!

• A piano is full of levers. Each key is a lever with other levers attached to it. When you press a key, the levers make hammers fly at the strings.

Body levers

The lower bones in your arm form a third-class lever with the pivot at your elbow. The muscle at the front of your upper arm is called the biceps. It makes the effort to lift up a weight in your hand, which is the load.

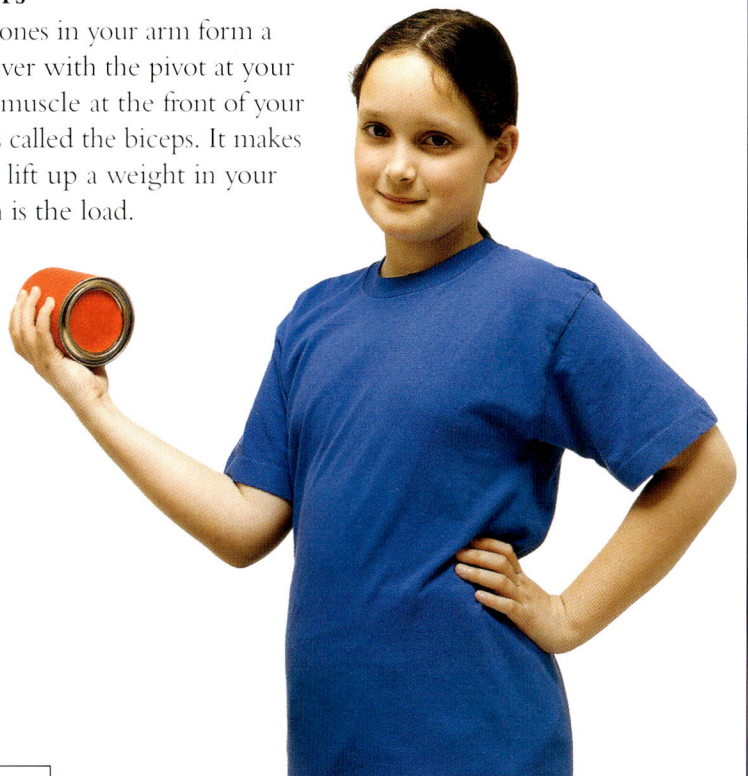

Your arm makes a third-class lever. As it lifts up an object, the effort is between the pivot and the load.

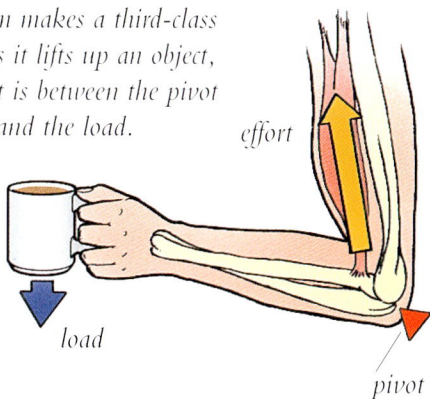

MAKING LEVERS WORK

MAKE A GRIPPER

You will need: *short pencil, two pieces of wood each about 15cm long, thick elastic bands, objects to pick up or squash such as sweets or grapes.*

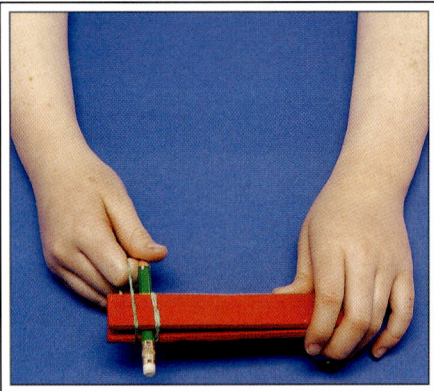

You can find out how to make two different lever machines in the projects here. The first is a simple gripper for picking up or squashing objects. It can act both as a pair of nutcrackers (a second-class lever) or a pair of tweezers (a third-class lever). In a pair of nutcrackers, the load (in this case a sweet) is between the pivot (the pencil) and the effort (where you push). In a pair of tweezers, the effort is between the pivot and the load. Draw a lever diagram that shows both ways of using lever machines to help you understand how each one works.

The second machine is a balance scale. It is like the ones used by the Romans about 2,000 years ago. It works by balancing the weight of an object against a known weight, in this case a bag of coins. The coins are moved along the lever arm until they balance the object being weighed. The further away from the pivot the weighted bag is, the greater turning effect it has on the lever arm. The heavier the weight being measured, the further the bag must be moved to balance the arm. The weight is read off against the scale along the arm.

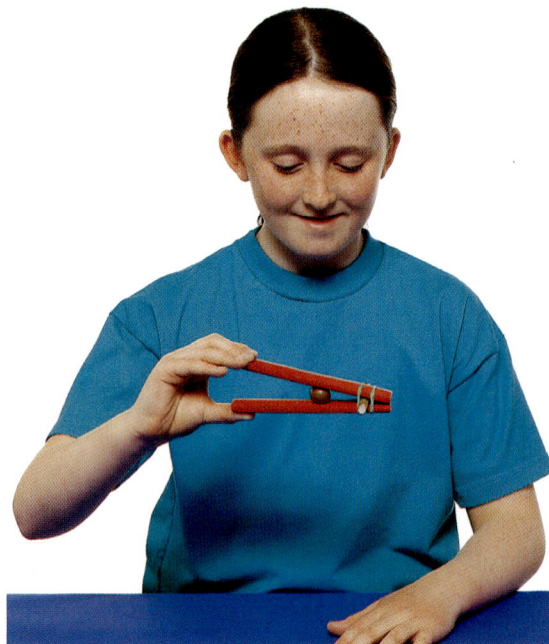

1 Put the pencil between the two pieces of wood, near one end. Wrap the elastic bands tightly around the pieces of wood to make a pivot. You have now made the gripper.

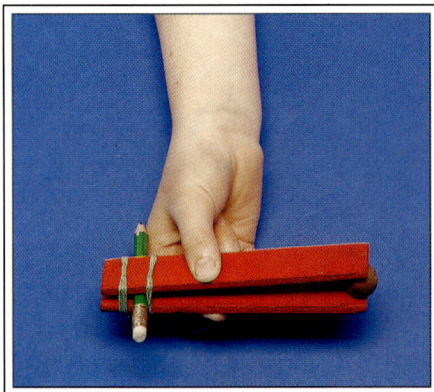

2 Hold the gripper near the pivot to make it act like a pair of tweezers. See if you can pick up a delicate object, such as a sweet or a grape, without crushing the object.

3 Holding the gripper at the other end makes a pair of nutcrackers. It increases the force you make. Try using the nutcrackers to crack a small nut or to crush a small sweet.

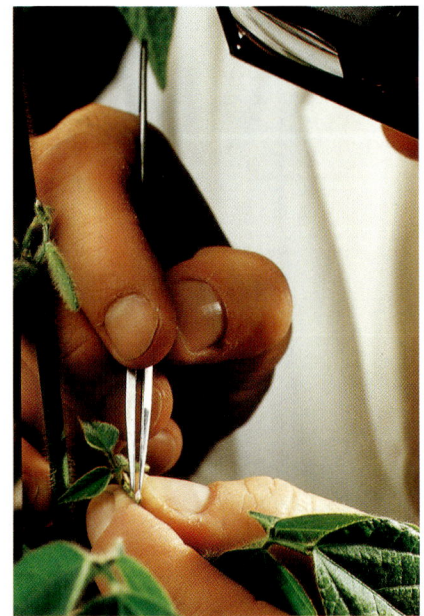

Gently does it
A pair of tweezers is used to pick up minute grains of pollen. Tweezers make it easier to pick up tiny or delicate objects. The tweezers act as a third-class lever, so the force that squeezes the object is smaller than the effort you use.

74

MAKE A BALANCE SCALE

You will need*: thick card about 50cm x 8cm, thin card, scissors, string, ruler, hole punch, 12-cm circle of card, sticky tape, 100g of coins, felt-tipped pen, objects to weigh.*

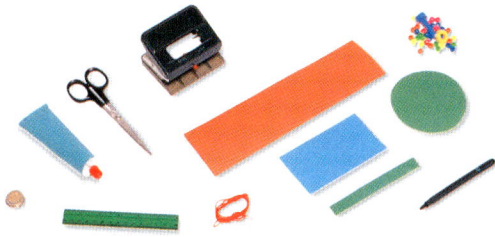

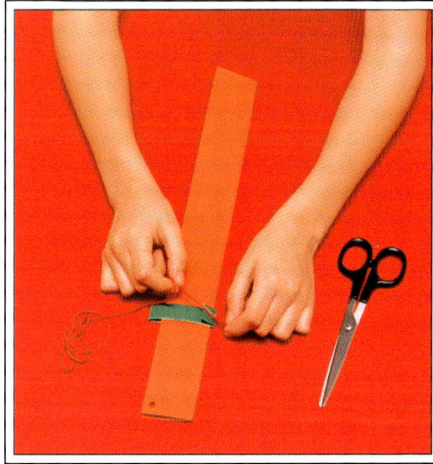

1 Make the arm by folding the thick card in two. Make a loop of thin card and attach it to the arm so that its centre is 11cm from one end. Tie a piece of string to this support.

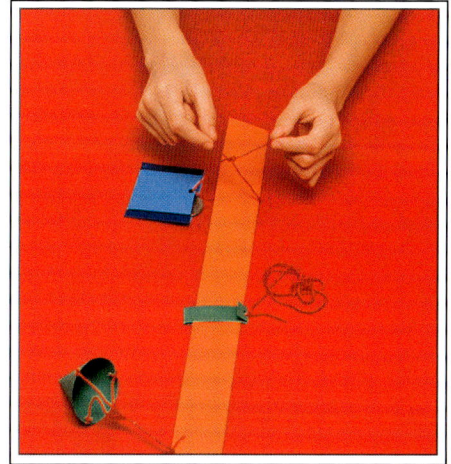

2 Make a hole 1cm from the arm's end. Make the card circle into a cone-shaped pan and tie it to the hole. Make an envelope and tie it to a loop so that it hangs over the arm.

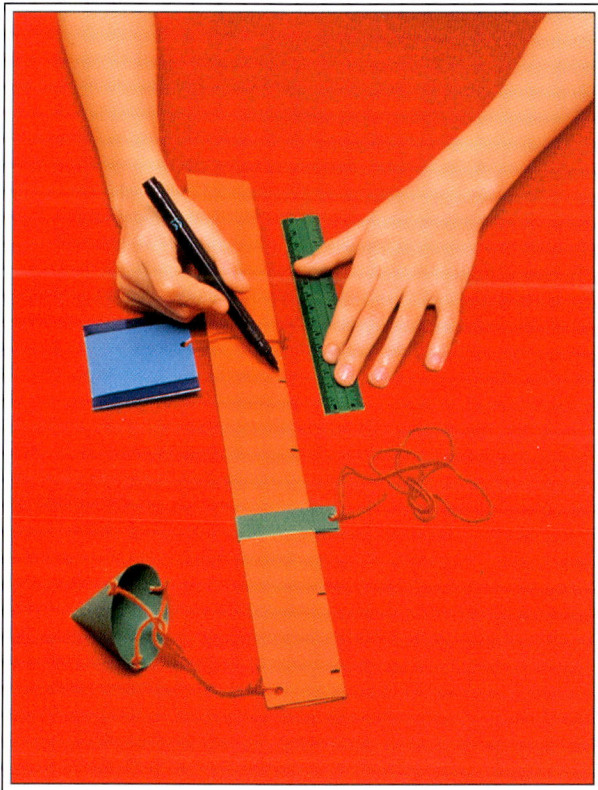

4 To weigh an object, put it in the pan and slide the envelope of coins backwards and forwards along the arm until the arm balances. Each mark along the scale equals 50g. In this picture, the object being weighed is about 75g.

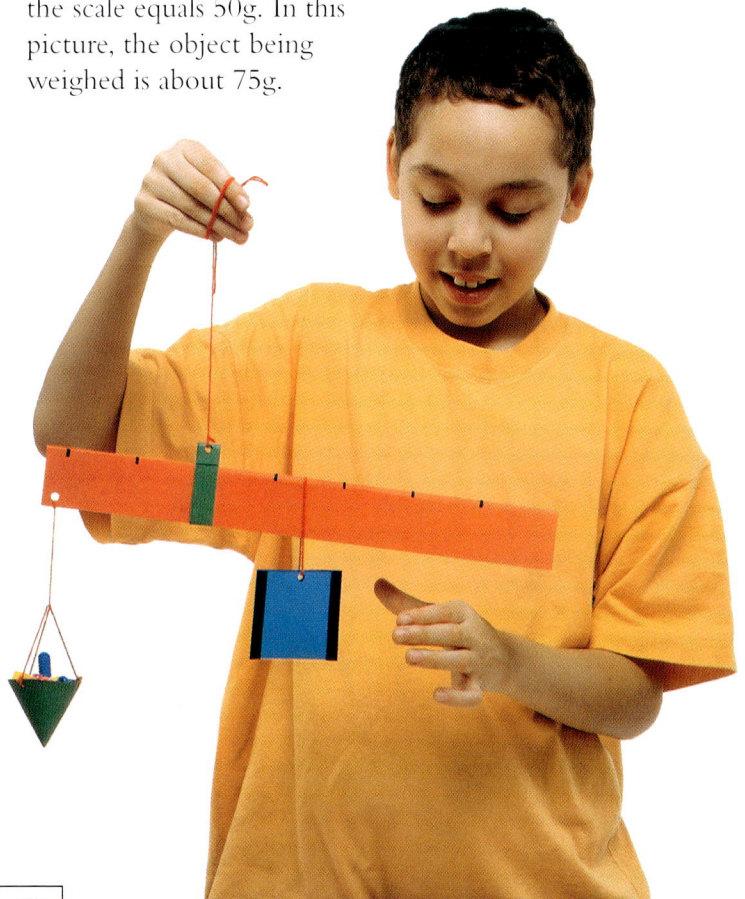

3 Put the 100g of coins in the envelope and seal it up. Starting from the centre of the support, make a mark every 5cm along the arm. This scale will enable you to work out the weight of any object you put in the pan.

WHEELS AND AXLES

The wheel is one of the most important inventions ever made. About 6,000 years ago, people discovered that using logs as rollers was a more efficient way to move heavy loads than to drag them. A slice from a log was the first wheel. Then people found that they could attach a wheel to the end of a pole. The pole became an axle.

A wheel on the end of an axle makes a simple machine. Turning the wheel makes the axle turn, too. It is a machine because turning the axle is easier using the wheel than turning the axle on its own. Wheels and axles increase mechanical advantage – turning the wheel makes the axle turn with greater force. The bigger the wheel compared to the size of the axle, the greater the force, making turning even easier. Wheels are used in millions of machines. One of the most obvious is in wheeled vehicles, which were in use more than 4,000 years ago and are still the most common form of transport today. Sometimes wheel and axle machines can be difficult to recognize. Can you find a wheel and axle in a spanner or a door key?

Pedal pusher
Pushing on the pedals of this child's tricycle turns the axle and drives the tricycle's front wheel.

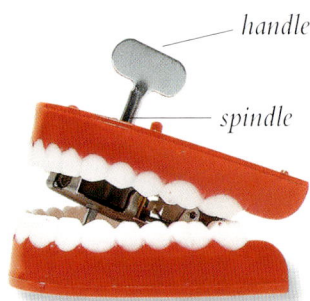

handle

spindle

Winding up
The key of a wind-up toy has a handle that acts as a wheel and a spindle that is an axle. The large handle makes it easier to turn the spindle.

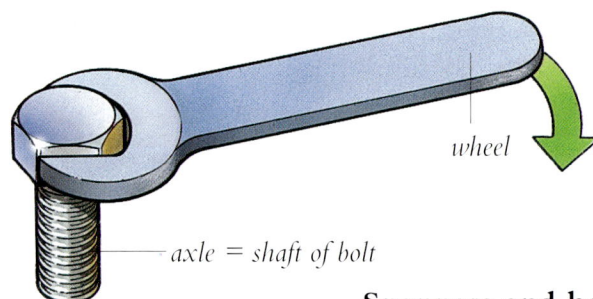

wheel

axle = shaft of bolt

Spanners and bolts
A spanner and a bolt make up a wheel and axle system. The threaded shaft of the bolt is the axle and the handle of the spanner is the wheel. By turning the spanner, it is much easier to tighten or loosen the bolt.

Lock and key
A key doesn't look like a wheel and axle machine, but it is. A key has a small handle on the end which makes it easier to turn in the lock. The handle acts as a wheel. The key's shaft is the axle.

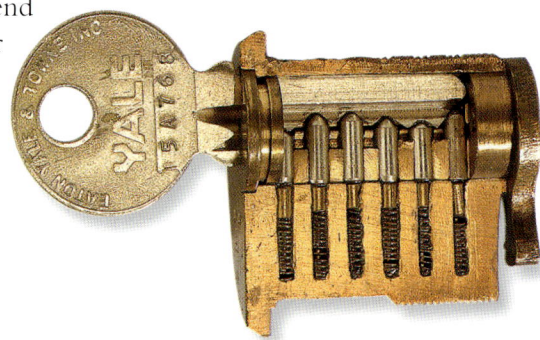

Putting the spoke in

A cart full of grapes is pulled by oxen in this Roman mosaic, which was made about 1,700 years ago. Using wheeled carts meant oxen could pull a much heavier load than they could carry. The first cart wheels were made from slices of tree trunk. About 4,000 years ago, the Romans hollowed the wheels out and added spokes to make them lighter. Vehicles could now go faster.

Potter's wheels

A potter in India uses a wheel to shape his pots. Making pots was one of the first uses of the wheel. Simple potter's wheels are still used around the world. The massive wooden wheel can be turned either by foot or by hand.

Keep on spinning

The rim of this grinding wheel moves at very high speed as it sharpens tools. The wheel is very heavy, which means that it tends to keep spinning even when the tool is pressed against it.

Racing wheels

A racing car is moved along by its rear wheels (which are called the driving wheels). Each driving wheel is turned by an axle called a driveshaft. In most cars the driving wheels are the front wheels.

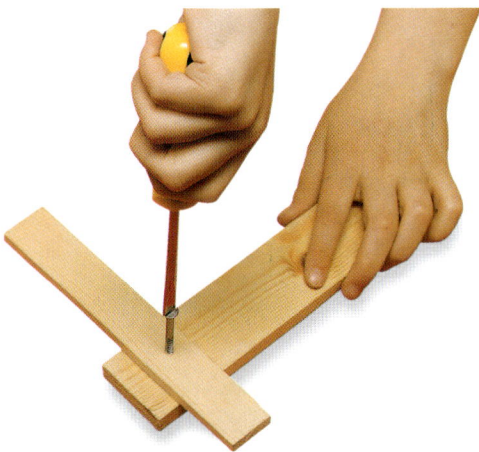

Driving in a screw

A screwdriver is a machine. Its shaft is an axle and its handle is a wheel. The handle increases the force on the shaft when it is turned to drive in a screw.

Steering wheels

A car's steering wheel is attached to the end of an axle, called the steering column. The wheel increases the force from the driver's hands, so giving the driver enough force to control the car.

WHEELS AT WORK

MAKE A CAPSTAN WHEEL

You will need: pencil, small cardboard box such as a shoe box, ruler, card tube, scissors, dowelling, sticky tape, string, a weight, thin card, glue, thick card.

There are hundreds of different examples of wheels and axles. Some are very old designs, such as the capstan wheel. A capstan is a wheel on an axle with handles that stretch out from the edge of the wheel. The handles are used to turn the wheel, which turns the axle. Large capstan wheels can be turned by animals as they walk round and round, or by several people who each push on a handle. In the past, they were a familiar sight on ships and in dockyards where they were used to raise heavy loads such as a ship's anchor. This project shows you how to make a simple capstan wheel for lifting a weight. At the end of the project a ratchet is attached to the axle. A ratchet is a very useful device that acts like a catch. It prevents the capstan wheel turning back on itself once you have stopped winding it.

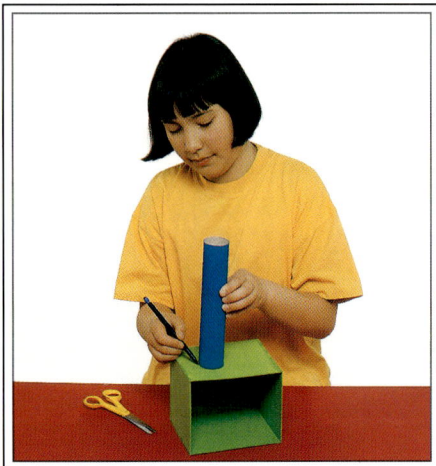

1 Draw a line around the box about one-third from the top. Place the tube on the line, draw around it and cut out a circle. Repeat on the opposite side of the box, so the circles match.

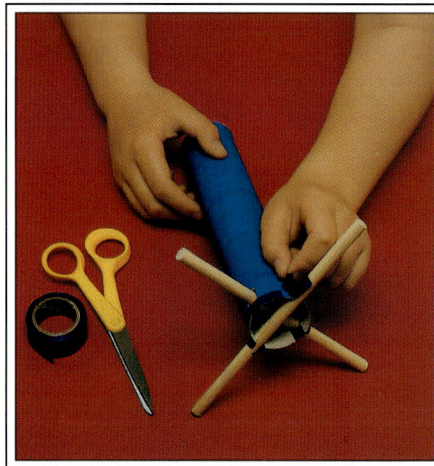

2 Cut four slots in one end of the tube. Lay two pieces of dowelling into the slots so that they cross over. Tape the dowelling in place. You have now made the capstan wheel.

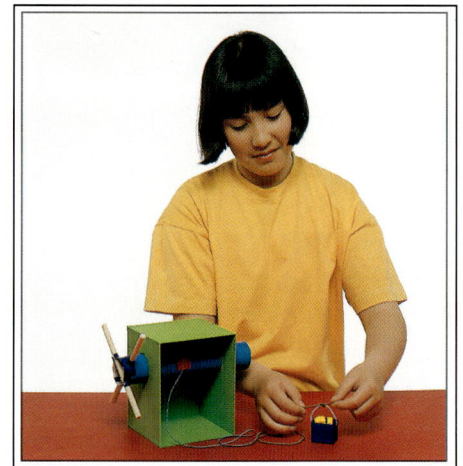

3 Push the tube into the holes in the box. Tape the end of a piece of string to the middle of the tube inside the box. Tie a heavy object to the other end of the string.

Round in circles
Sailors on board a sailing ship turn a capstan wheel. The wheel turns a drum that pulls the ship's heavy anchor up from the sea bed. The longer the handles on the capstan wheel, the easier it is to turn the drum, but the farther the sailors have to walk. Pulling up the anchor by hauling in the cable would be far more difficult.

78

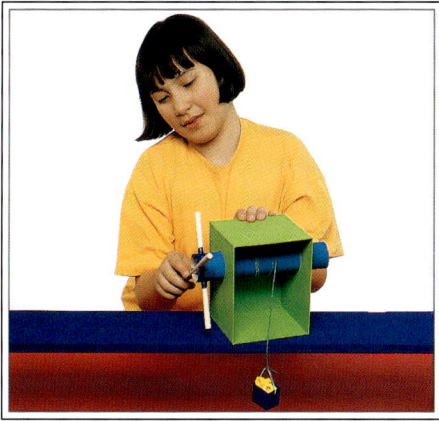

4 Stand the box on a table edge so the weight hangs down. Turn the capstan wheel to lift the object. Try turning the handles at their ends and then near the wheel's centre.

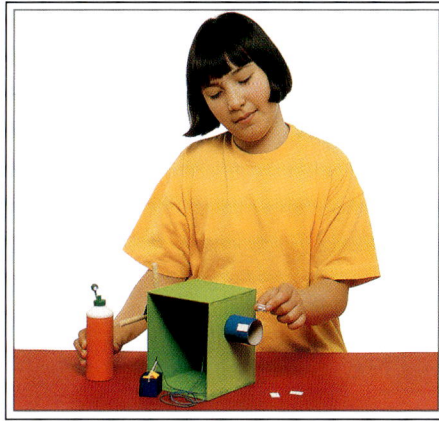

5 To make a ratchet, cut four small rectangles of card and carefully glue them to the tube at the opposite end to the capstan wheel. These will form the ratchet teeth.

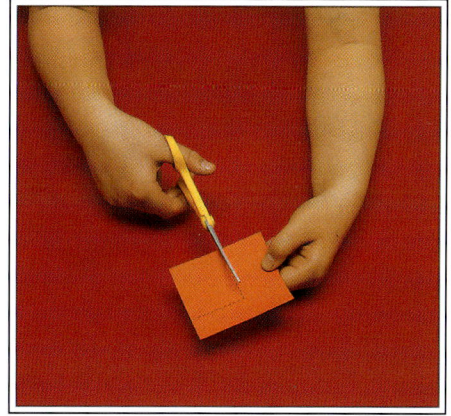

6 From a piece of thick card, cut an L-shaped piece. Bend one of the legs of the L at a right angle to the other leg. This will form the part that locks into the ratchet teeth.

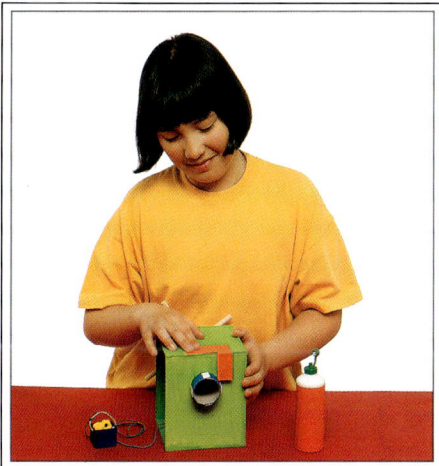

7 Glue the L card to the top of your box so that the end hanging over the edge just catches in the ratchet teeth. Leave the glue to dry before trying your ratchet.

8 Wind up the capstan wheel to lift the weight up again. You should now be able to let go of the capstan without the weight dropping back to the ground. The teeth will catch on the L shape, stopping the axle from turning backwards.

Crushing the grapes

A wine press crushes grapes from a vineyard to release the grape juice that is used for wine-making. The press is operated by turning a nut at the top that forces a screw thread downwards into the tub. The horizontal bar on the nut works like a capstan. Pushing in opposite directions on its ends turns the nut. The longer the bar, the greater the turning force on the nut, and the greater the squashing force on the grapes.

SLOPING RAMPS

How can an inclined plane, or ramp, be a machine? It is a type of machine because it makes going uphill, or moving an object uphill against the force of gravity, much easier. Think about a removal van and people trying to lift a heavy box inside it. It might take two people working together to lift the box up high enough to reach into the van. One person could push the box up a gently sloping ramp on his or her own.

Ramps are useful in many different situations. You often see ramps on building sites, and stairs are ramps, too. The shallower (less steep) the slope, the easier it is to move an object up it, but the further the object must move to gain the same amount of height. For example, when you are walking uphill on a zig-zag path you are using ramps. Walking along the gently sloping sections of the path is easier than walking straight up the steep hillside, but you have to walk much further to reach the top. Railways have to use winding routes to go up hills because trains cannot get up very steep hills without sliding backwards.

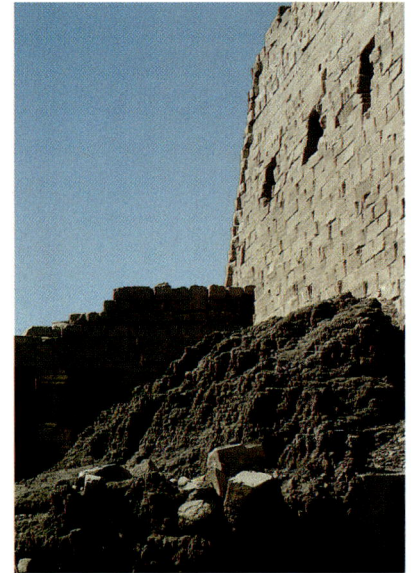

Mud-brick ramp
These are the remains of a ramp made of mud bricks. The ramp was built by the ancient Egyptians about 3,000 years ago. Egyptian pyramid and temple builders had no cranes. They used ramps to move building materials up to where they were needed.

Steep slope
A large effort is needed.

Shallow slope
A small effort is needed.

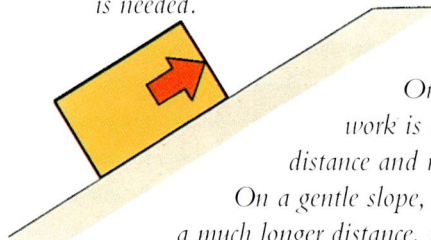

On a steep slope, all the work is done in a short distance and needs a large effort. On a gentle slope, the work is done over a much longer distance, making it easier.

Ramps for building
A ramp is being used to construct a building in this picture, which was copied from an ancient Egyptian tomb painting. Without construction machines such as cranes, the Egyptians had to build huge sloping ramps to pull stone blocks to the upper levels of the building.

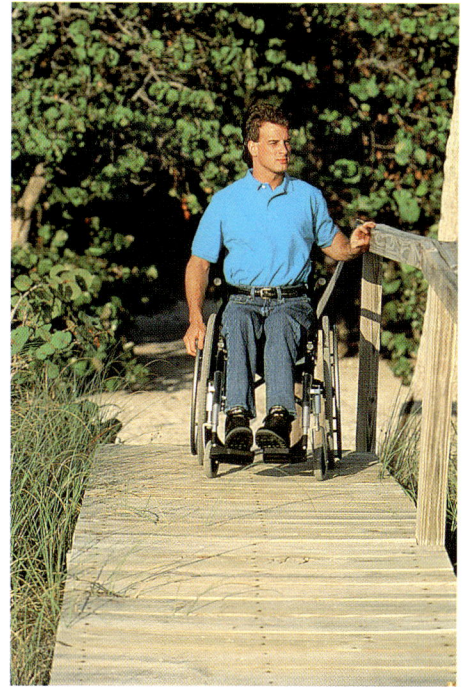

Ramps for loading

A car is driven up a ramp on to the back of a delivery truck. Long, gently sloping ramps are easier to drive up than short, steep ones. Loading and unloading cars from a transporter truck is easy using ramps because the cars can be driven on and off the truck. No winches or cranes are needed.

Fast track

When engineers plan roads such as motorways, they try to avoid steep carriageways. Cuttings and embankments are built into hillsides to provide gentle slopes. Vehicles are able to climb the slopes without having to slow down too much.

Access ramps

A disabled man is using a ramp to get down to the beach. Ramps make it much easier for vehicles with wheels to travel from one level to another. Many public buildings, such as libraries, sports centres and hospitals, often have ramps leading up to their doors as well as steps. Without ramps, people with wheelchairs or push-chairs often find it difficult to get in and out of buildings.

Zigzag roads

Mountain roads, such as this one in South Africa, zigzag upwards in a series of gentle slopes. A road straight up the side of the valley would be far too steep for most vehicles to drive up.

FACT BOX

• Most canals have flights of locks to move boats up and down hill, but a few use inclined planes, or ramps. In a 1.6km-long inclined plane in Belgium, the boats float inside huge 5,000-tonne tanks of water. The tanks are hauled up the inclined plane on rails.

• The railway line from Lima to Galera, in Peru, climbs 4,780m. In some places the track zigzags backwards and forwards across the very steep hillsides.

WEDGES AND SCREWS

A pair of scissors and your front teeth have something in common. They are simple machines called wedges that use inclined planes (ramps) to work. A wedge is a type of ramp, or two ramps back-to-back. Pushing the thin end of a wedge into a narrow gap with a small effort makes the wedge press hard on the edges of the gap, forcing the gap apart. Chisels, axes and ploughs all work with wedges. If you look closely at their blades you will see that they widen from the cutting edge.

Screw threads are also a type of inclined plane. Imagine a long, narrow ramp wrapped around a pole. This is what a screw thread is. Screw threads make screws, nuts and bolts and car jacks work. It only takes a small effort to turn a screw thread to make it move in or out with great force. Screw threads provide a very secure way of fixing something together, or of raising a heavy load.

Wedging a door
A door wedge stops a door from opening or closing. Pulling on the door pulls the bottom of the door further up the wedge's ramp. This makes the wedge press even harder against the bottom of the door and the floor.

Wedges as cutters
An axe is used to cut down a tree. The axe head is wedge-shaped. When it hits the wood, its sharp edge sinks in, forcing the wood apart and splitting it. The handle allows the person operating the axe to swing it with great speed and lever out pieces of wood.

Wedges for woodworking
Wedges are useful for shaping materials. The axe in the foreground uses a wedge to split wood. The woodworker in the background is using a small wedge-shaped tool to remove small amounts of material from the wood, which is spun at high speed by a foot pedal.

Digging with screws
The screw-shaped tool in this picture is called an auger. It is used to dig deep holes for fence posts, or for filling with concrete, to make secure foundations for buildings. The auger is operated by a mechanical digger. The auger both loosens soil from the bottom of the hole and transports the soil to the surface.

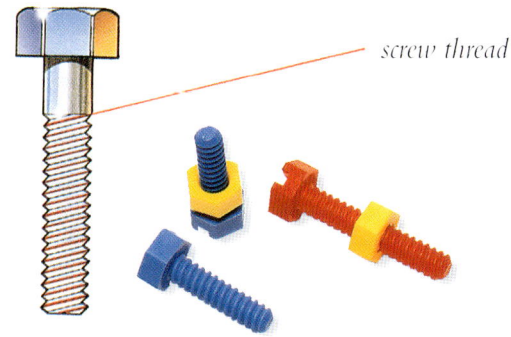

Screws

A screw uses a screw thread to attach itself firmly into wood or metal. A screw thread is a ramp wrapped around a pole. Turning the thread is like moving up or down the slope.

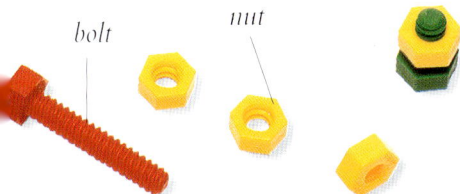

screw thread

Nuts and bolts

A nut and bolt are used to join objects together. The screw threads on the nut and bolt interlock so that turning the nut makes it move down the bolt.

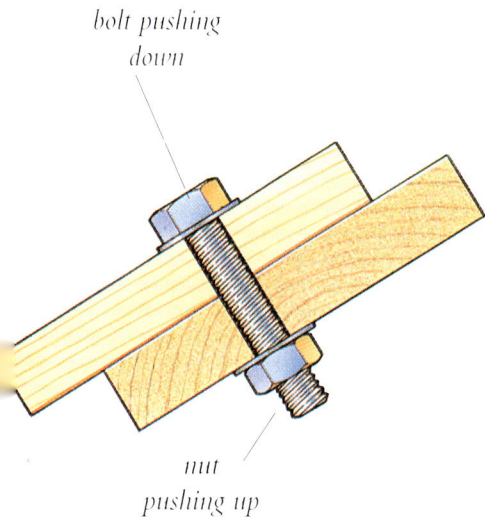

bolt

nut

bolt pushing down

nut pushing up

When the nut is screwed on to the bolt the combined force of the nut and bolt squeezes the two pieces of wood tightly together.

Spiralling slope

A corkscrew has a screw thread that makes it wind into a cork as the handle is turned. The screw only moves a small way into the cork for each turn of the handle. This makes winding the corkscrew quite easy.

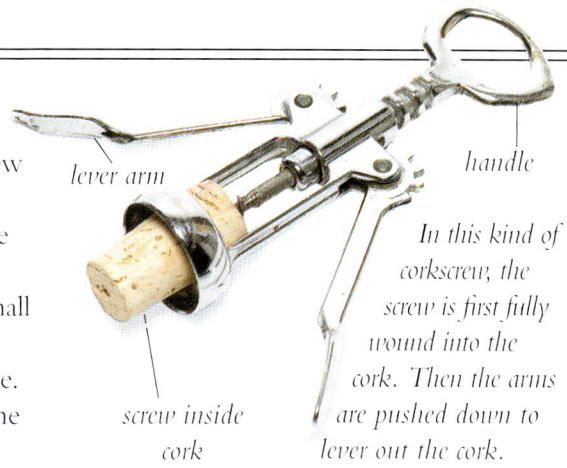

lever arm

handle

screw inside cork

In this kind of corkscrew, the screw is first fully wound into the cork. Then the arms are pushed down to lever out the cork.

Uncorking a bottle

A corkscrew such as this one combines three simple machines: the wheel and axle, the wedge and the lever. The handle of the corkscrew acts as a capstan to make turning in the screw easier. One end then folds down to rest on top the bottle's neck, and the other end forms a lever for pulling out the cork.

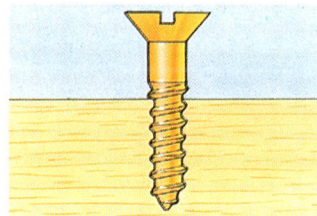

The point of a wood screw helps it to sink into the wood. The thread makes the point go in deeper as the screw is turned.

Driving force

Using a screwdriver increases the force with which you can turn a screw. As it turns, the screw thread bites into the wood. The screw is also wedge-shaped to help it force its way into the wood. Using screws is a strong and secure way of fixing all sorts of materials together.

PLANES AT WORK

Although screw threads are most commonly used for joining things together, they can also be used to lift a weight upwards. In a screw jack, the force made by turning the screw thread is used to lift a weight upwards. With a screw jack, a huge weight, such as a car, can be lifted easily, but slowly. One turn on the handle of the jack using a small effort raises the heavy load a few millimetres.

The first project on these pages shows you how to make a simple type of screw jack. The second project shows you how to make a device to measure force, or the effort needed to raise an object. Use it to compare how a gentler slope makes lifting an object easier.

handle

bar

screw thread

MAKE A SCREW JACK

You will need: *long bolt with two nuts, a washer, strong glue, piece of wooden board or thick card, lolly stick or short piece of wood, cardboard tube, card, a weight to lift.*

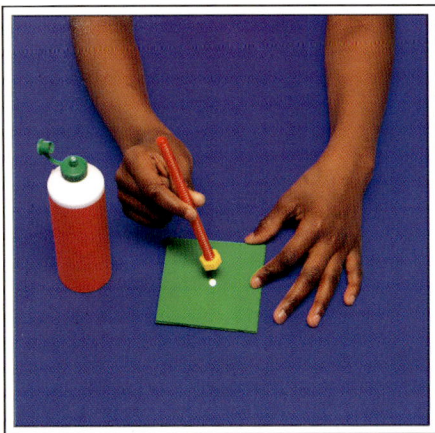

Squashing with screws
The apple press uses a screw to squash the juice from apples. Turning the screw is quite easy, but it makes a huge force for squashing the apples.

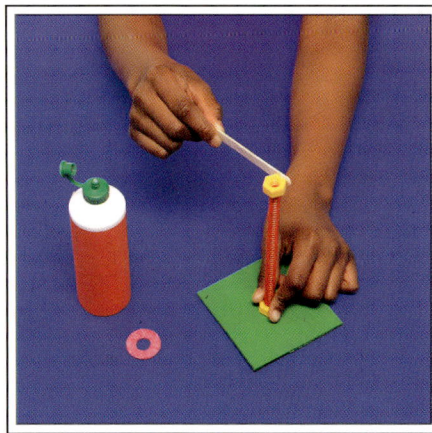

Lift up
If a car gets a puncture, the driver can lift the car with a screw jack before changing the wheel. The driver places the jack on the ground with the bar underneath the car. As the driver turns the handle, the bar moves up the screw thread and lifts the car.

1 Fix a nut on one end of the bolt. Glue the bolt to the middle of a square piece of wooden board or thick card so that the thread is pointing upwards. Leave to dry.

2 Glue the end of the lolly stick to the side of a nut (the nut must fit the bolt) to make a handle. When the glue is dry, wind the nut on to the bolt and put the washer on top.

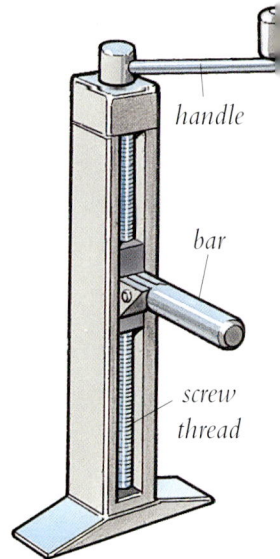

3 Stick the tube to a rectangle of card. Place tube over the bolt so it rests on top of the washer. Move a weight up and down by turning the handle on the nut.

MAKE A FORCE MEASURER

You will need: *piece of wood or thick card, elastic band, paper fastener, string, pencil or felt-tipped pen, ruler, model vehicle, materials to make a slope (such as a plank and books).*

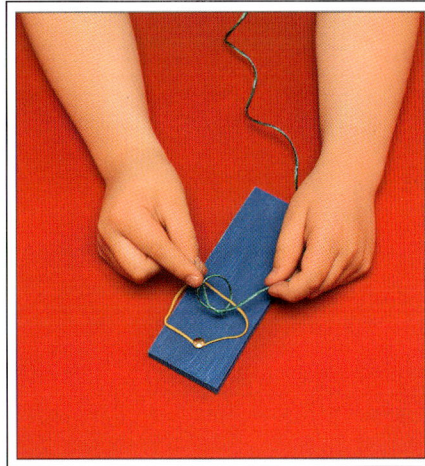

1 Measure and cut a piece of wood or card about 15cm x 5cm. Attach the elastic band near one end with a paper fastener. Tie a piece of string to the other end of the band.

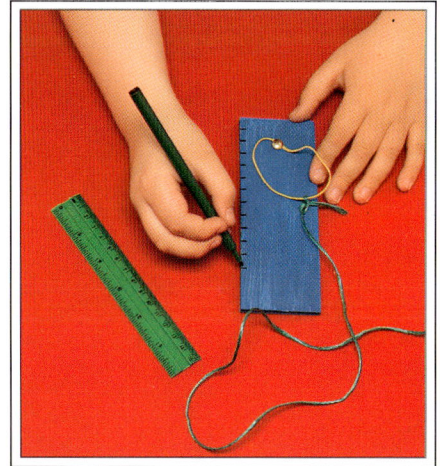

2 Mark centimetres along one edge of the wood, for recording how far the elastic band stretches when it is pulled by the weight. You have now made your force measurer.

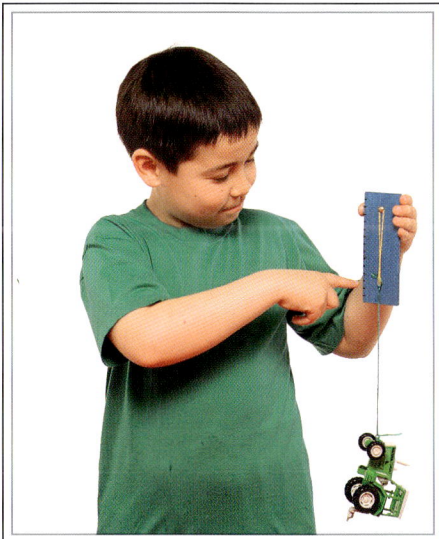

On a level
The ancient Egyptians used ramps to lift huge stone blocks to build their pyramids. As the building progressed, more ramps were added so that they were always level with the top of the building.

3 Use your force measurer to find the weight of the model vehicle. Hang the model from your measurer and note where the band stretches to. Write down the measurement.

4 Make a slope – try using a plank propped up on books. How much force is needed to pull the vehicle up the slope? Is it less or greater than the model's weight? Try again with a shallower slope. Does the force needed change? You should see that it needs less force to pull the model vehicle up the shallower slope.

LIFTING WITH PULLEYS

Using a pulley is often the easiest way to lift a heavy load high up. The pulley is a simple machine. The most basic pulley system is a wheel with a groove in its rim in which a rope is fitted. The wheel rotates around an axle. The rope hangs down either side of the wheel, with one end attached to a load. Pulling down on the rope lifts the load hanging on the other end. It does not reduce the amount of force needed to lift an object, so there is no mechanical advantage. It does, however, make lifting the load easier, because it is easier to pull down than it is to pull up. A pulley's special advantage is that it changes the direction of the force.

Using several pulleys together makes lifting even easier and many pulley systems have more than one wheel that operate together. A pulley system such as this is called a block and tackle. Pulleys are useful for lifting loads on building sites and dockyards, and for moving heavy parts and machinery in factories.

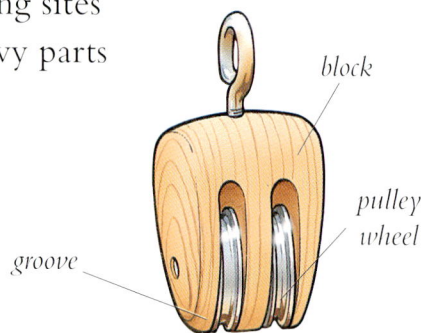

block

pulley wheel

groove

A block and tackle has two blocks like the one shown above, arranged one above the other. The pulley wheels are designed to turn easily as the rope runs around them, through the groove.

Pulling down

The simplest pulley system is a single pulley wheel with a rope running over it. It changes the direction of the pull (the effort) needed to lift an object (the load) off the ground. Instead of pulling up on the object, the boy is pulling down on the rope. He can use his weight to help.

Winching with pulleys

An air-sea rescue helicopter uses an electric winch to lift sailors from the sea on the end of a wire. The wire runs from the winch over a pulley wheel on the side of the helicopter.

Pulleys for building

Workmen use a pulley to lift building materials to construct the walls of a great city in the 1500s. The workman at the bottom turns a handle to haul up the bucket. The pulley was probably devised by ancient Greeks about 2,500 years ago and has been in use ever since.

Half the effort

This pulley system has two pulley wheels. Pulling the rope raises the lower wheel and the load. With two wheels, the effort needed to lift the load is halved. This makes it easier, but the rope has to be pulled twice as far.

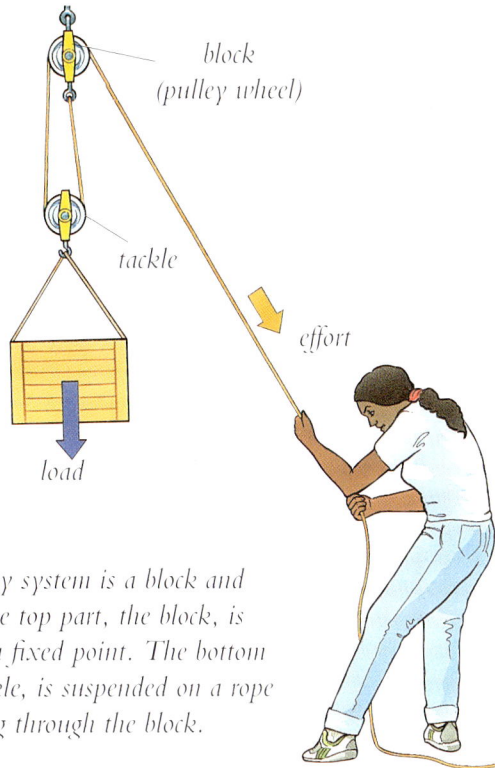

block (pulley wheel)

tackle

effort

load

This pulley system is a block and tackle. The top part, the block, is attached to a fixed point. The bottom part, the tackle, is suspended on a rope passing through the block.

Up and away

A light pull on a loop of chain lifts a very heavy boat engine. This pulley system has a very high mechanical advantage – it takes little effort to pull a massive weight.

Dockyard block and tackle

The lower end of the block and tackle on a dockyard crane can be seen in this picture. The crane is lifting heavy pallets of cargo from the deep hold of a ship.

Boats away!

A ship's lifeboats hang on pulley systems ready to be lowered quickly into the sea if the ship has to be abandoned. The pulley systems allow the heavy boats to be lowered by one person standing inside the boat itself.

Higher and higher

A dockyard crane uses pulley systems to lift very heavy loads. The cable from the pulley is winched in and out by an engine to make the lifting hook rise and fall. Other engines move the crane's arm up and down.

PULLEYS AT WORK

The two projects on these pages illustrate how pulley systems work. In the first project, a simple double pulley system is constructed. It does not have pulley wheels. Instead, the string passes over smooth metal hoops. This would be no good for a real system because friction (a force that slows things down) between the rope and metal would be too great, but it does show how a pulley system is connected together.

The second project investigates how adding more turns on a block and tackle reduces the effort needed to move a load. You may notice, however, that the more turns you make, the greater the friction becomes. Using wheels in a block and tackle cuts down this friction.

Lifting materials
Construction cranes make use of pulleys to lift heavy materials to the upper floors of a building. Pulleys make the hook move up and down and backwards and forwards along the crane's boom.

MAKE A SIMPLE PULLEY

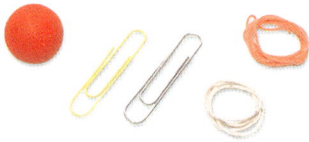

You will need:
lengths of string,
two large paper clips,
a weight.

Linking up
Heavy-duty block and tackle systems, like this one in a dockyard, are used for lifting the heavy cargo. They have metal chain links, which are much stronger than a rope would be. The chain links interlock with the shaped pulley wheels.

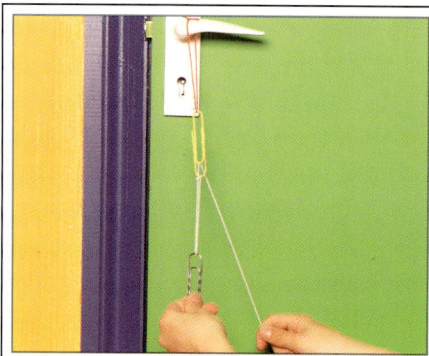

1 Take a short length of string. Use the string to tie a large paper clip to a door handle, or coat hook fixed to a wall. Make sure the paper clip is tied securely to its support.

2 Cut a long piece of string and feed it through the paper clip's inner hoop. Now feed it through the top of a second paper clip and tie it to the outer hoop of the top clip.

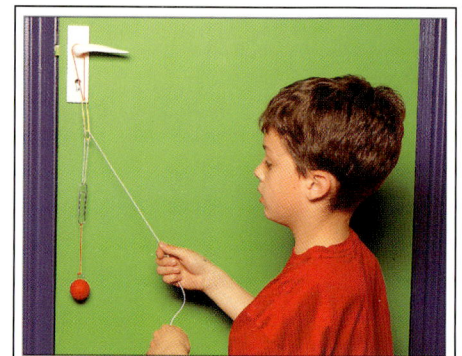

3 Fix a weight, using another piece of string, to the bottom paper clip. Pull the end of the long string to lift the bottom paper clip, which will lift the weight.

MAKE A BLOCK AND TACKLE

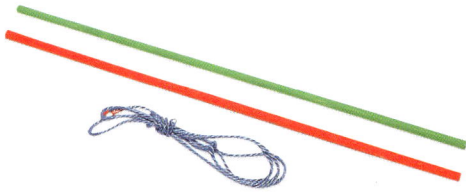

You will need:
*two broom handles or
lengths of thick dowelling,
strong string or thin rope,
two friends.*

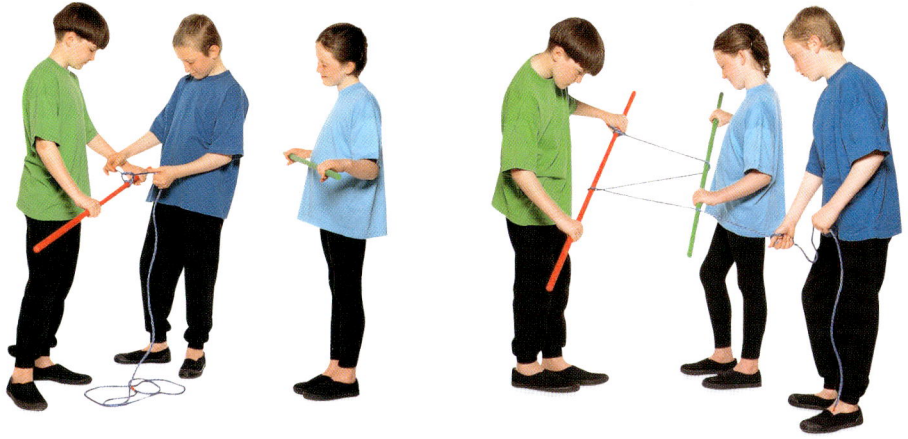

1 Ask each of your friends to hold a broom handle, or length of dowelling, between outstretched hands. Tie the end of a long piece of string, or rope, to one handle.

2 Wrap the string around each handle once, keeping the loops fairly close together on the handles. Now pull on the string. How easy was it to pull your friends together?

FACT BOX

• Using a block-and-tackle system with a mechanical advantage of 20 (with ten wheels at each end), you could lift an elephant easily by hand!

• One of the first people to make use of block and tackle systems was the famous Greek scientist Archimedes. He is said to have pulled ships ashore with them, in the third century BC.

---

3 Now wrap the string twice around each handle, making sure you keep the turns close together. Now pull on the end of the string again. What differences do you notice this time? Is it any easier?

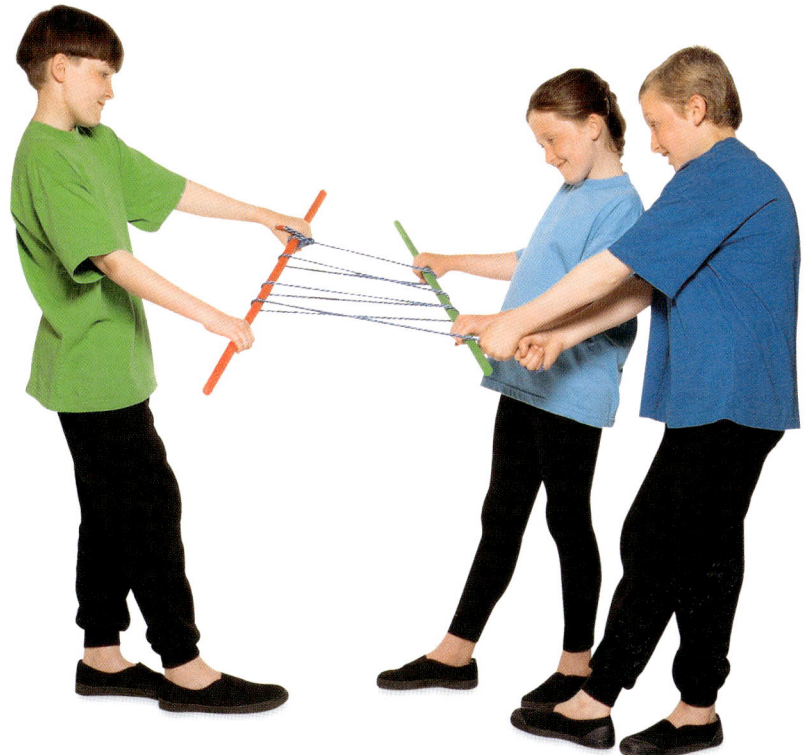

4 Make more turns around the handles and try pulling again. Do more turns make the effort you need to make smaller? Do you have to pull the rope farther than before?

GEAR WHEELS

A gear is a wheel with teeth around its edge. When two gear wheels are put next to each other their teeth can be made to interlock. Then when one wheel turns, the other one turns, too. Gears are used to transmit movement from one wheel to another. If both wheels are the same size, the wheels turn at the same speed. If one wheel is bigger than the other, the gears can be used to speed up or slow down movement, or to increase or decrease a force. Many machines, from kitchen whisks to trucks, have gears that help them to work.

Belt drives and chain drives are similar to gears. In these, two wheels are linked together by a belt or a chain instead of teeth. This is another way of transferring power and movement from one wheel to another. Speed can also be varied by changing the size of the wheels.

Tooth to tooth
This is a simple gear system. One gear wheel turns the other because the teeth interlock with each other. The larger wheel will make the smaller wheel turn faster because it is bigger, so the smaller wheel takes less time to turn a full circle. The larger wheel is twice the size of the smaller one.

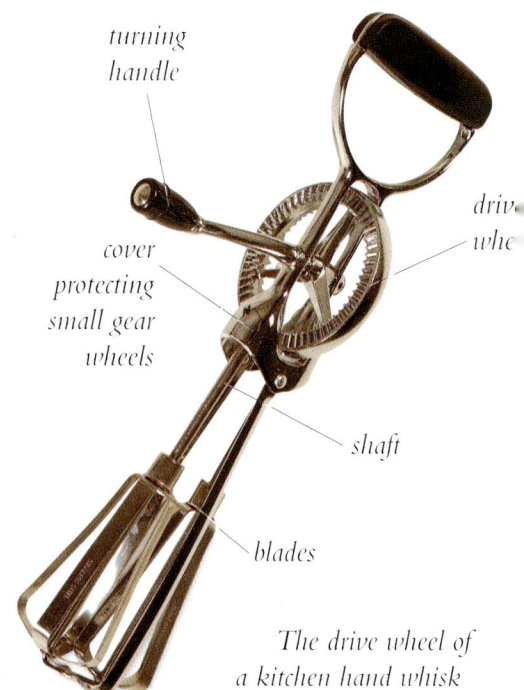

Mining with gears
Huge gear wheels are part of an old lift mechanism from a mine. The teeth on the interlocking gear wheels press very hard against each other. They need to be very wide and thick so that they don't snap off.

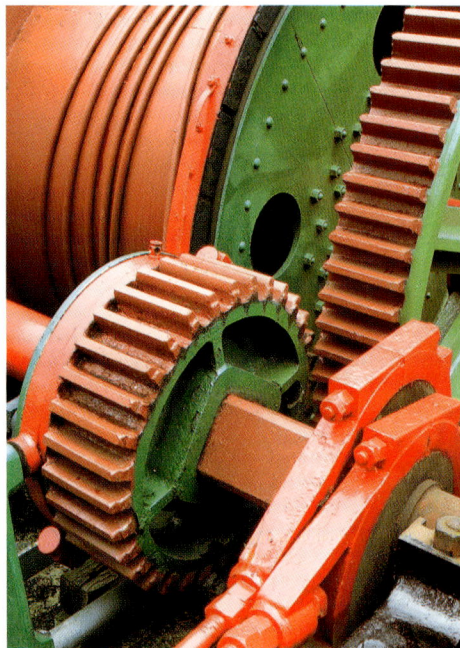

turning handle

cover protecting small gear wheels

driv whe

shaft

blades

Transmitting a force
In the centre of this kitchen whisk is a set of gears. They are used to transmit the turning movement of the handle to the blades of the whisk. The gears speed up the movement, making the blades spin faster than the turning handle. The gears turn the movement through a right angle, too. These sort of gears are called bevelled gears.

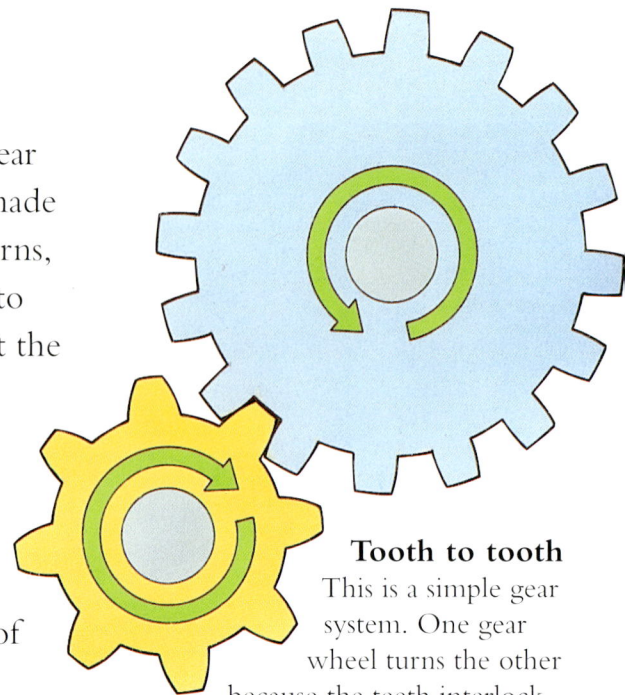

The drive wheel of a kitchen hand whisk transmits the motion of the handle to the smaller gear wheels attached to the shafts. The smaller gears turn much faster than the larger drive wheel and in the opposite direction to each other.

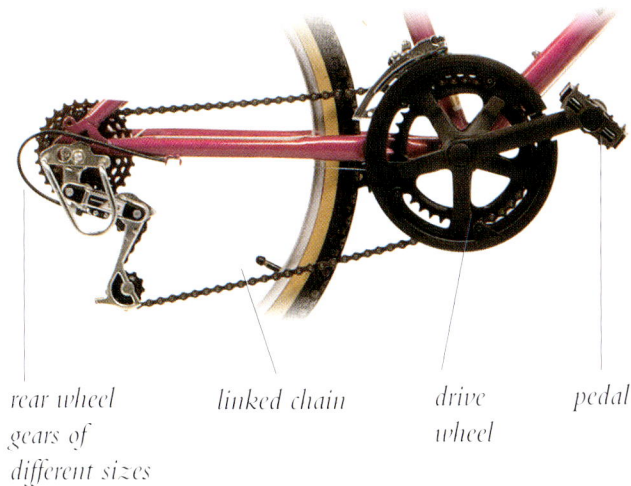

All geared up

Bicycle gears use wheels and a chain to transmit the drive from the pedals to the bicycle's rear wheel. As a rider turns the pedals, the drive wheel is moved around. This moves a linked chain, which turns a set of gear wheels of different sizes attached to the rear wheel. With the chain on the largest of these gears (in low gear), pedalling is easy but the bicycle travels slowly. With the chain on the smallest gear (in high gear), pedalling is harder but the bicycle moves faster.

rear wheel gears of different sizes

linked chain

drive wheel

pedal

interlocking gears

winder to wind up spring

Wind-up watch gears

The back has been removed from this wind-up watch so you can see the tiny gear wheels inside. Different-sized gear wheels are arranged so that they move the hands of the watch at different speeds. The clock is powered by a spring, wound up by hand. The spring makes a gear wheel turn, which moves the minute hand. Another gear slows down this movement to turn the hour hand.

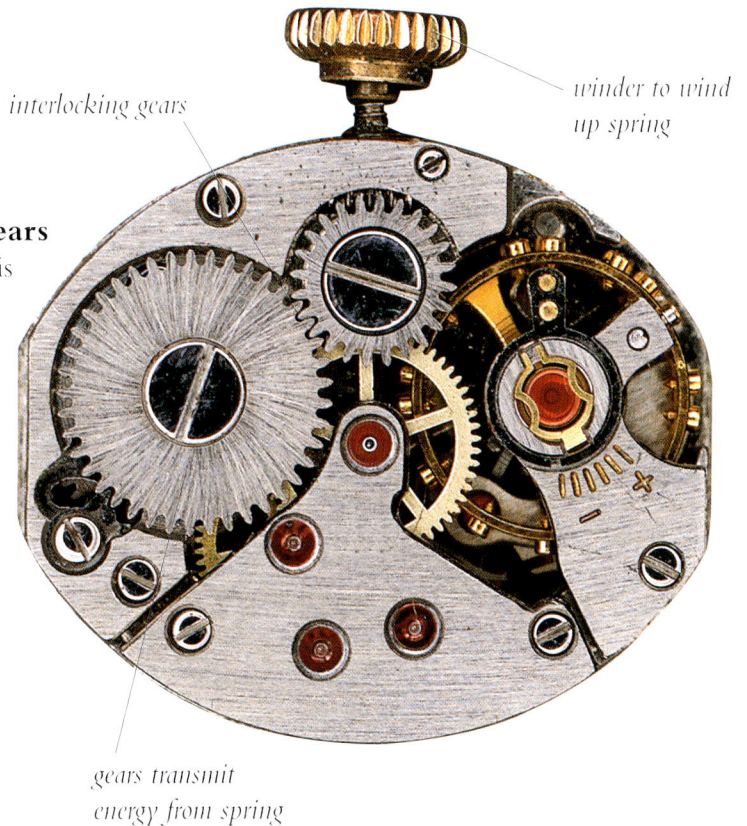

gears transmit energy from spring

Swinging time keeper

This pendulum clock uses gear wheels to control its speed. A spring drives one gear round, which drives other gears that show time. The speed that gears turn at is controlled by a swinging pendulum that interlocks with the teeth on a gear wheel called the escape wheel. The escape wheel gives the pendulum a small push on each swing to keep the pendulum moving.

Belt drives

Wide belts, called belt drives, stretch between wheels in the roof and the machines of a factory. The photograph was taken in about 1905. The wheels in the roof are turned by an engine, and the belts transmit this movement to drive the machines.

MAKING GEARS WORK

Before engineers used metals, they made gear wheels from wood. One way of making gear-wheel teeth was to fix short poles on to the edge of a thick disc. The poles on different gear wheels interlocked to transmit movement. Gears like this were being used 2,000 years ago. If you visit an old mill, you might still see similar wooden gears today. The first project shows you how to make a simple gear wheel system. What do you notice about how the wheels turn? They turn in different directions and the smaller wheel (with fewer teeth) turns one and a half times for every one rotation of the larger wheel. The second project shows you how to make a simple belt drive and how it can turn an axle at different speeds.

Slow pedal power
Old sewing machines, such as this one, were powered by a foot pedal that turned a large pulley wheel. This wheel was linked by a drive belt to a small pulley wheel on the machine. So pedalling slowly made the small wheel turn quickly.

MAKE A SET OF GEAR WHEELS

You will need: *pair of compasses and pencil, protractor, thick card, scissors, used matchsticks or thin dowelling, glue, paper fasteners, small cardboard box.*

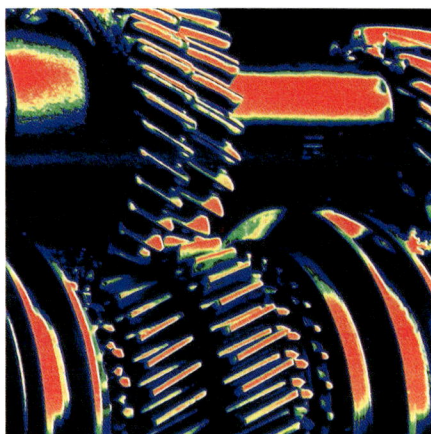

Spiral gears
A computer graphic image shows part of a car gear box. These gears are helical (spiral) gears, which are more efficient than gears with straight teeth.

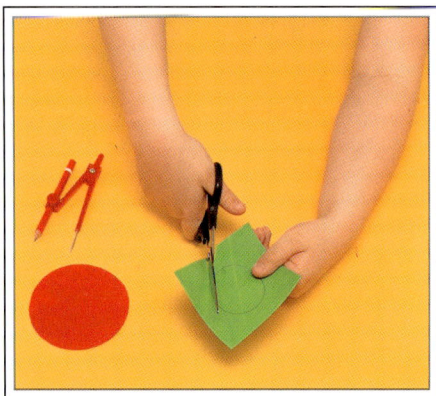

1 Using a pencil and compasses, mark out two discs on card and cut them out. Make the diameter of one disc twice the diameter of the other, for example 8cm and 4cm.

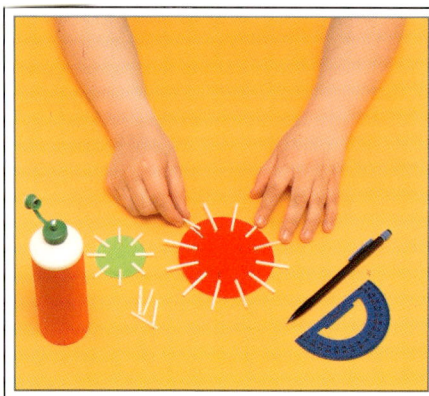

2 Glue eight matches around the edge of the small disc. First glue four matches in a cross shape, then add four more half-way. In a similar way, glue 12 matches to the large disc.

3 Use paper fasteners to attach one wheel to the top of the box and the other to the side so that the teeth interlock. Turn one disc to turn the other.

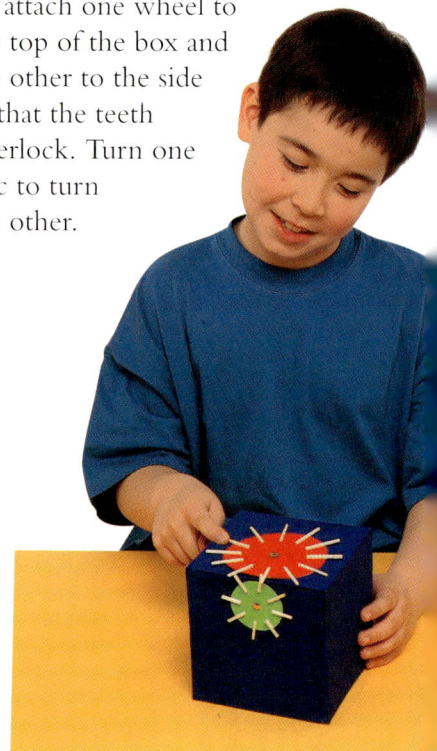

MAKE A BELT DRIVE

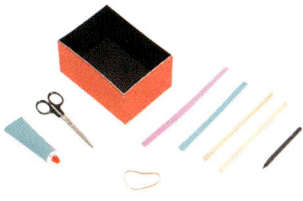

You will need: *cardboard box, dowelling, scissors, strips of thin card, glue, thick elastic band, felt-tipped pen.*

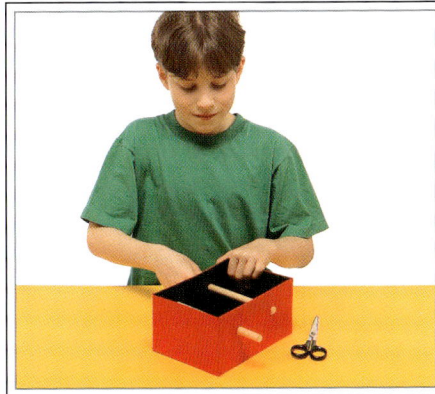

1 Cut two pieces of dowelling each about 5cm longer than the width of the box. Cut two holes in both sides of the box. Slide the dowelling through to make two axles.

2 Cut a strip of card. Glue it to one of the axles. Wrap it round and glue the end down to make a wheel. Make a bigger wheel with a strip of card three times longer than the first.

3 Put a wide elastic band around both axles. The band should be slightly stretched when it is in place. Make a mark at the end of each axle so you can see how fast they turn.

Printing gear
Computer printers use gears driven by electric motors to move sheets of paper past the print head (where the ink is fired onto the paper) bit by bit at the correct speed. More gears move the print head from side to side, making up lines of the image.

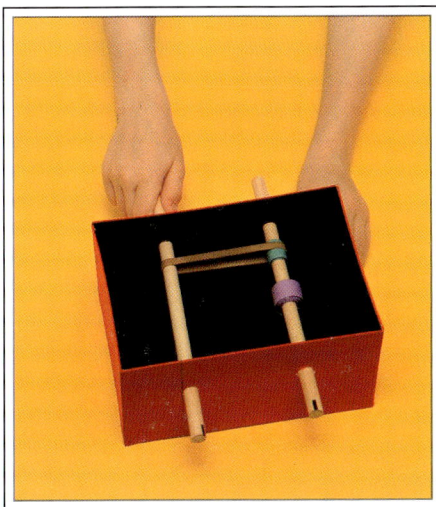

4 To test your belt drive, put the elastic band on to the smaller wheel and start turning the plain axle. Does the wheeled axle turn more or fewer times than the plain?

5 Now move the elastic band on to the larger wheel and start turning the plain axle again. What difference does it make to the speed of the wheeled axle? Use the pen marks to compare the speeds.

POWER FOR MACHINES

Early machines, such as axes and ramps, relied on human muscle power to make them work. Then people started using animals to work many simple machines. Animals, such as oxen, can carry, pull and lift much heavier loads than people can. Eventually people realized they could capture the energy of the wind or flowing water by using windmills and water-wheels. These became the first machines to create power that in turn was used to make other machines work. This energy was used to do such things as grinding grain to make flour or pumping up water from underground.

Today, wind and water energy are still captured to generate electricity, which we use to light and power our homes, schools, offices and factories.

Wind for milling

A windmill uses the power of the wind to turn heavy mill stones that grind grain to make flour. The whole building can be turned around so that the sails are facing into the wind. The speed of the mill is controlled by opening and closing slots in the sails.

Power walking

A man is operating a treadmill in Australia in the 1840s. He is walking up the rungs so that his weight turns the wheel. The movement of the wheel is used to operate machinery. Human treadmills are no longer used.

Overshot water-wheel

There are two different types of water-wheel. This one is called an overshot wheel because the water flows over the top of the wheel and falls into buckets on the wheel. The water's weight pulls the wheel around.

Undershot water-wheel

The second type of water-wheel is called an undershot wheel because rushing water in a stream or river flows under the wheel and catches in the buckets at the bottom of the wheel. The force of the water spins the wheel.

Grinding stones

Many windmills and watermills generate power to turn millstones. The grinding stones in this picture are used to squeeze oil from olives. Only the top millstone turns while the bottom stone stays still.

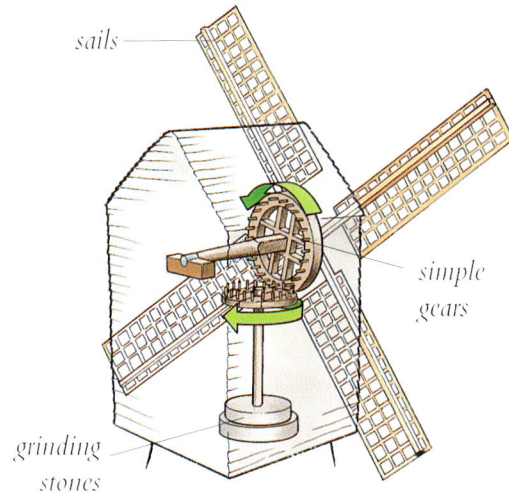

sails

simple gears

grinding stones

Inside a windmill is an arrangement of wooden gear wheels, which transfers power from the sails to the grinding stones. Mills like this have been in use for centuries.

Modern mills

Wind turbines, like these shown on a wind farm, are a modern type of windmill. The wind spins the huge propellers, which turn an electricity generator inside the top of each turbine.

Power from water

A hydroelectric station generates electricity from the water of a fast-flowing river. The water is stored behind a huge dam. As it flows out, it spins a turbine, which is like a very efficient water-wheel. The turbine turns a generator, which makes electricity.

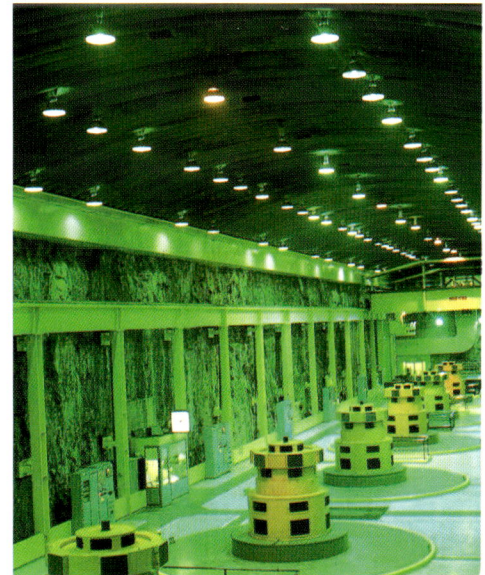

Underground power

In the underground turbine hall of a hydroelectric power station, each of the generators can produce about a gigawatt of electricity – enough electricity to work about 10 million light bulbs.

WIND AND WATER POWER

Modern windmills are called wind turbines and are used to generate electricity. The most efficient wind turbines only have two or three blades, as in the propeller of an aircraft. Hundreds of wind turbines can be grouped together to make a wind farm. Sometimes one or two large turbines generate enough electricity to power a small community. There are several shapes of wind turbine. One of the most efficient is the vertical-axis type. This has an axle standing vertical to the ground. It is very efficient because it works no matter which way the wind is blowing.

The first project shows you how to make a vertical-axis turbine. The second project shows you how to make an overshot water-wheel. This captures the energy of falling water to lift a small weight. Try pouring the water on to the wheel from different heights to see if it makes a difference to the wheel's speed.

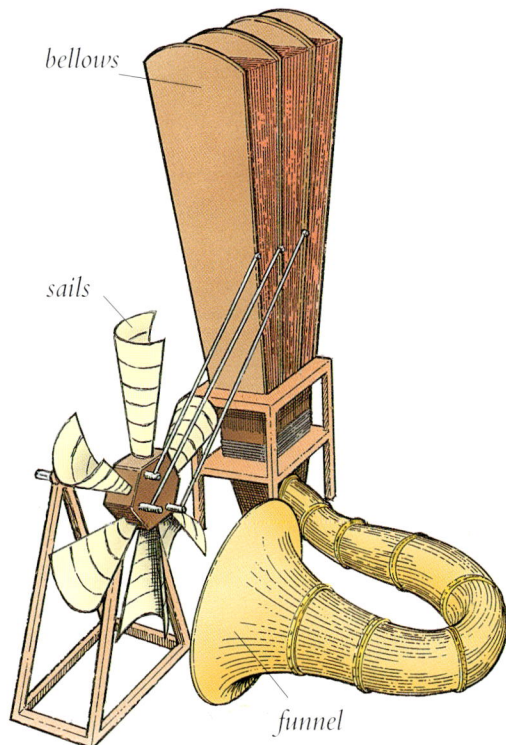

MAKE A WINDMILL

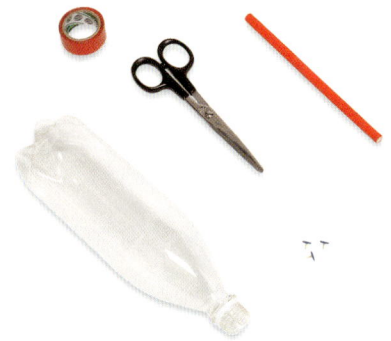

You will need:
plastic bottle, scissors, sticky tape, thin dowelling, drawing pins.

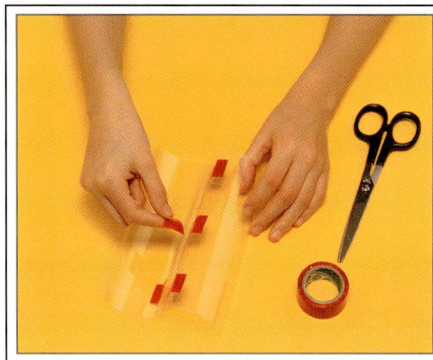

bellows

sails

funnel

Round and round again
This machine was devised in the 1500s by an Italian inventor. He believed that as the sails turned, they would operate a set of bellows. The bellows in turn would provide enough wind to drive the sails to set up a continuous cycle of movement. It cannot work because the sails do not provide enough energy to squeeze the bellows.

1 Cut the top and bottom off the bottle to leave a tube. Cut the tube in half lengthwise, then stick the two halves together in an S shape, so the edges overlap by 2cm.

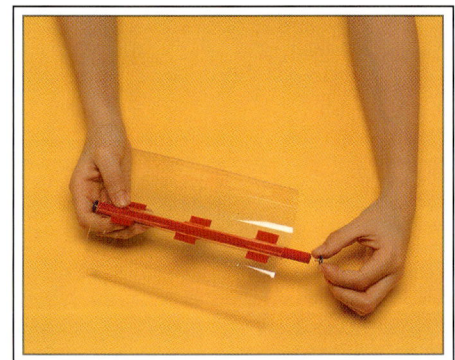

2 The piece of dowelling should be about 4cm longer than the vanes. Slide it into the slot between the vanes. Press a drawing pin gently into each end of the dowelling.

3 To make the windmill spin, hold it vertically with your fingers on the drawing pins at each end of the dowelling. Blow on the vanes. The windmill will spin easily.

MAKE A WATER-WHEEL

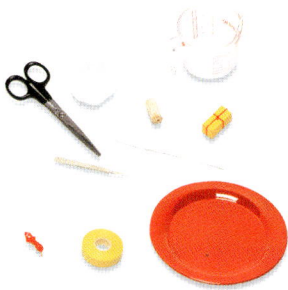

You will need: *large plastic bottle, scissors, wire (ask an adult to cut the bottom out of a coat hanger), cork, craft knife, sticky tape, string, weight, jug of water, large plate.*

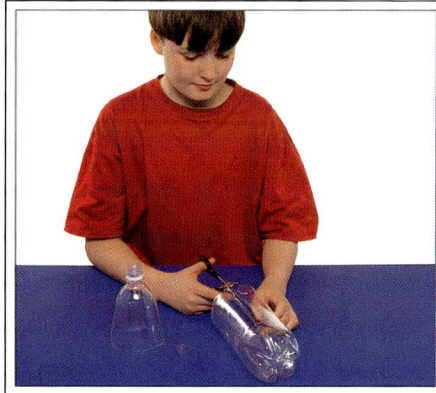

1 Cut the top third off the plastic bottle. Cut a small hole in the bottom piece near the base (this is to let the water out). Cut a V-shape on each side of the rim.

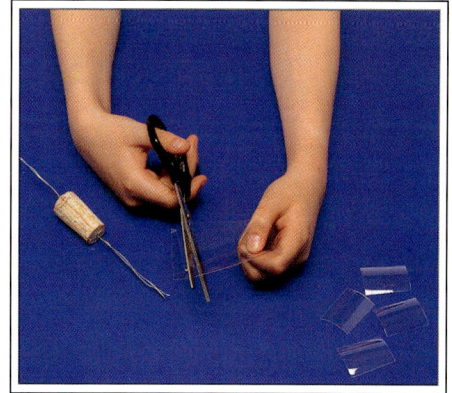

2 Ask an adult to push the wire through the centre of the cork to make an axle. From the top third of the plastic bottle, cut six small curved vanes as shown.

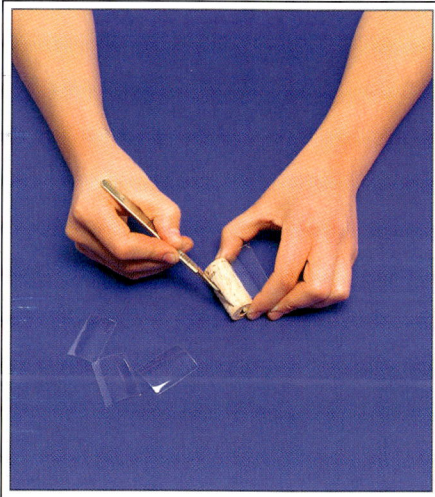

3 Ask an adult to cut six slots in the cork with a craft knife. (This might be easier without the wire.) Push the plastic vanes into the slots to make the water-wheel.

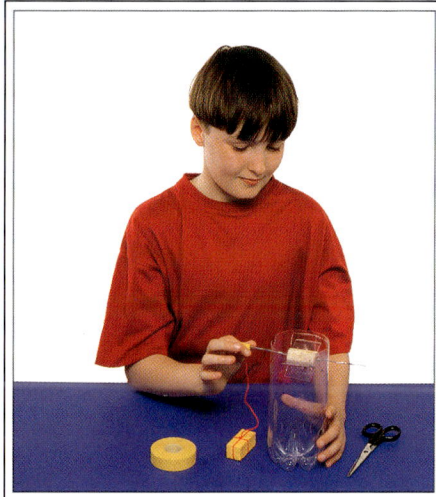

4 Rest the wheel's axle in the V-shaped slots. Tape a length of string towards one end of the axle and tie a small weight to the end of the string. Fill a jug with water.

FACT BOX

• In a strong breeze, the world's largest wind turbine, in Hawaii, USA, would be capable of operating more than 4,000 microwave ovens.

• China's Three Gorges Dam will generate 18 gigawatts of electricity – enough to work 24 million microwave ovens!

5 Put the water-wheel on a large plate or in the sink. Pour water on to the wheel so that it hits the upward-curving vanes. The weight should be lifted up.

Animal power

A water-raising wheel such as this one would be operated by an animal or a person walking in a circle, pulling the horizontal pole on the right. Buckets attached to a chain driven by the wheel go down into the well, scoop up water, lift it, and empty it into a chute.

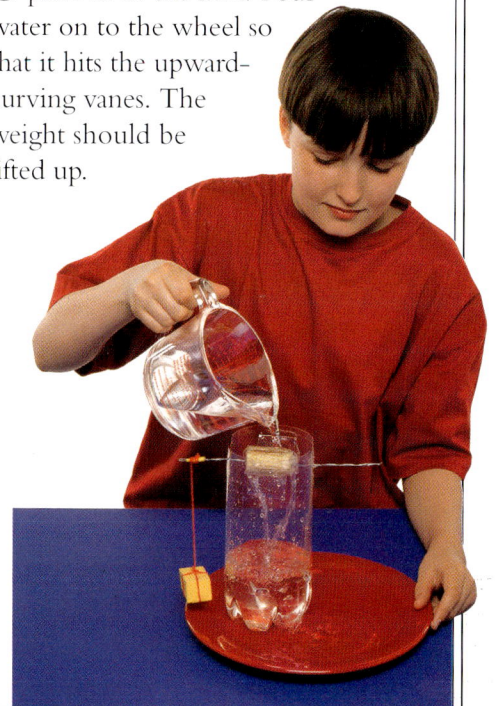

ENGINES AND MOTORS

Many modern machines are powered by engines and motors, which are complicated machines themselves. An engine is a machine that makes movement energy from heat. The heat is made by burning a fuel, such as petrol. The first engines were driven by steam.

Most engines today, such as the ones used in cars, are internal-combustion engines. This means that the fuel is burned inside the engine. In a car engine, as the petrol explodes, it produces hot gases that push pistons inside cylinders up and down. The pistons turn a crankshaft, which carries the movement energy from the engine to the wheels of the car. An electric motor is a machine that makes movement energy from electricity rather than from burning fuel. Most of the electricity we use is made in power stations or from the chemicals inside batteries.

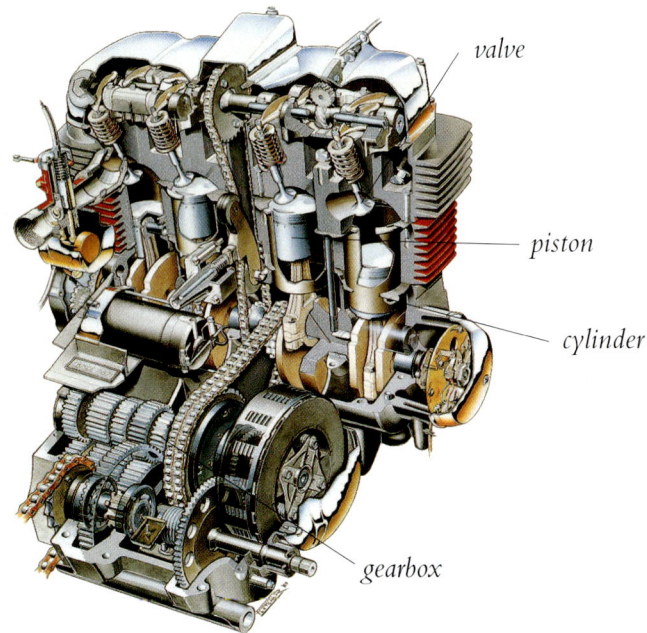

valve

piston

cylinder

gearbox

Burning inside
This diagram shows the pistons inside the internal-combustion engine of a car. At the top are valves that let fuel and air into the pistons and let exhaust gases out. At the bottom is the gearbox that sends the power from the engine to the wheels.

steam out

locomotive wheel

steam in

hinged link

cylinder

piston pushing out

Early steam power
An atmospheric engine was one of the first types of steam engines. Steam was fed to a cylinder, where it was cooled and turned back to water, forming a vacuum. The atmospheric pressure outside the cylinder pushed the piston in.

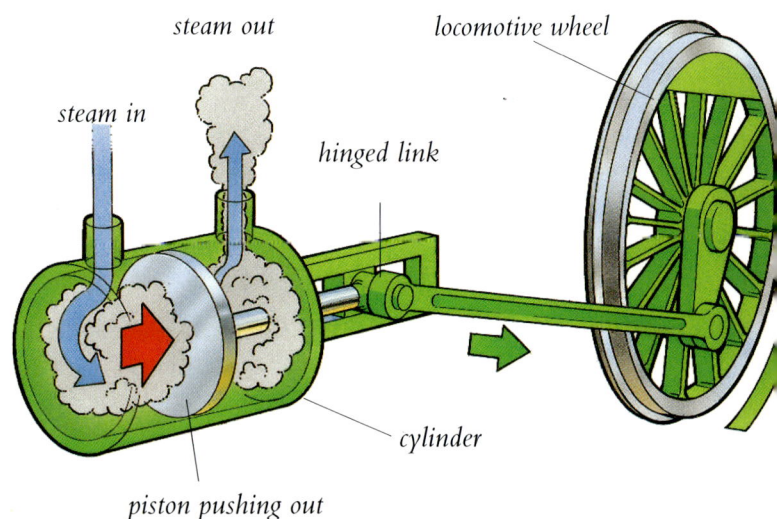

Piston power
In a steam engine, steam made by heating water in a boiler is forced along a pipe into a cylinder. The pressure of the steam pushes a piston in the cylinder outwards. The moving piston then turns a wheel that is used to drive a locomotive or power a machine.

Engines for cars

A car's internal-combustion engine is usually fitted under the bonnet. The engine's cylinders are inside the large black engine block. You can see the exhaust pipes that carry away waste gases from the cylinders.

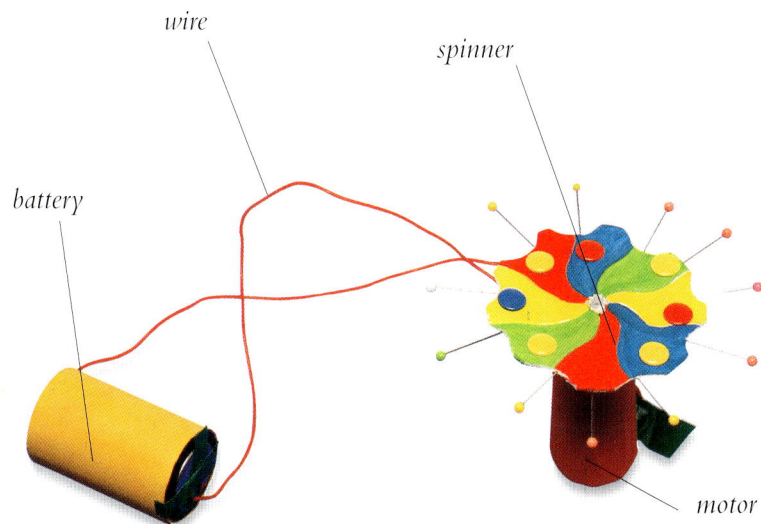

Under the bonnet

The top of an internal-combustion engine in a small truck. On the left are the starter motor (an electric motor that makes the engine turn to start it up) and the alternator, which makes electricity for the electrical parts of the truck, such as the lights.

Electric motors

Electricity is turned into movement by an electric motor. When the motor is connected to a battery, its shaft spins around. Electric motors are small and clean, which makes them useful for household gadgets.

wire

spinner

battery

motor

An electric motor with a colourful spinner on top is connected to a battery by two wires. This makes an electric circuit.

HYDRAULICS AND PNEUMATICS

Did you know that a machine can be powered by a liquid or a gas? Machines that have parts moved by a liquid are called hydraulic machines. Those that have parts moved by a gas are called pneumatic machines. A simple hydraulic system has a pipe filled with oil and a piston (a cylinder that moves to and fro) fitted at each end. Pushing one piston into the pipe forces the piston at the other end outwards, transmitting power from one end of the pipe to the other. In a simple pneumatic system, compressed air is used to force a piston to move.

Hydraulic and pneumatic machines can be very powerful. They are also quite simple and very robust. Machines that work in dirty and rough conditions, such as diggers, drills and tipper trucks, often have hydraulic or pneumatic systems instead of motors. Most dental drills are also worked by a pneumatic system. Air, pumped to the drill, makes a tiny turbine inside the drill spin very fast.

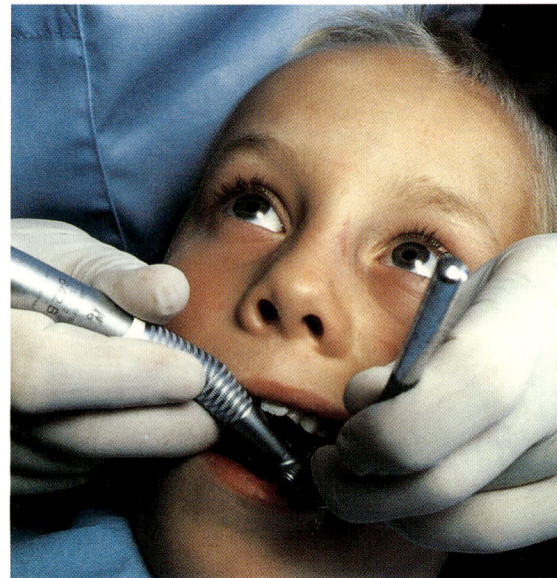

Dental drilling
The high-pitched whine of a dental drill is made by the air that powers it. Inside is an air turbine that spins an amazing 10,000 times a second as air is pumped through it.

Pump it up
Using an air pump is a simple way to blow up a balloon. A valve in the pump's outlet allows air to be pumped into the balloon as the piston is pushed in. It prevents the air being sucked out again when the piston is pulled out.

Lift it up
Pneumatic power can lift up a book. The girl blows air into the balloon and pushes the book upwards. The actual lifting takes less effort than lifting the book by hand – most of the effort is in stretching the balloon. Try this with an airtight, non-stretchy plastic bag.

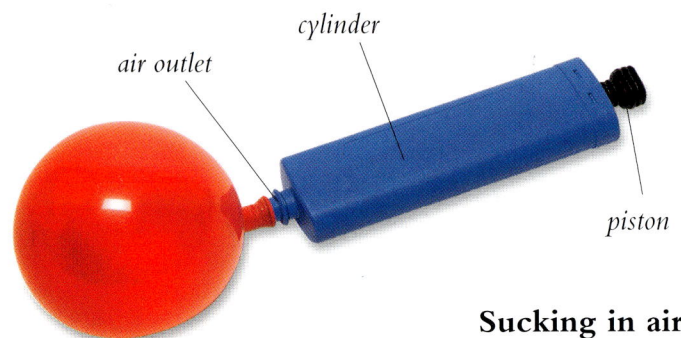

cylinder

air outlet

piston

Sucking in air
All pneumatic machines need a device to suck in air from the outside and push it into the machine. This is called an air pump, or a compressor. The simple air pump above sucks in air as the piston is pulled back, and forces air out as the piston is pushed in.

Hydraulic lift

Lifting and moving a heavy load is made easy with a hydraulically-powered machine such as a fork-lift truck. The forks are lifted by hydraulic rams. Each ram consists of a fixed cylinder and a piston that moves inside it. Pumping special oil, called hydraulic fluid, into the cylinder makes the piston move in or out, depending on which end of the cylinder the oil is pumped into.

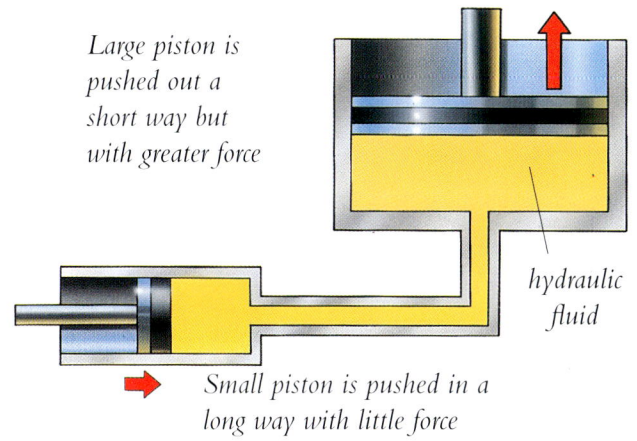

Large piston is pushed out a short way but with greater force

hydraulic fluid

Small piston is pushed in a long way with little force

Pushing in, pushing out

A simple hydraulic system has two pistons connected by a cylinder filled with hydraulic fluid. Using different-sized pistons creates a mechanical advantage. Pushing the small piston creates a greater force at the large one.

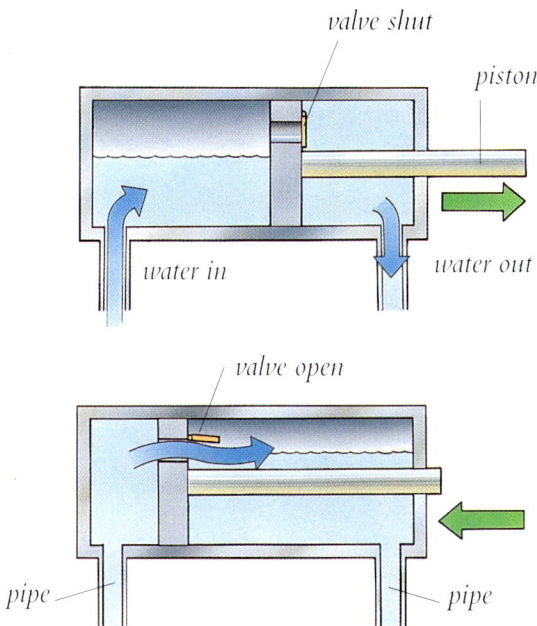

valve shut

piston

water in

water out

valve open

pipe

pipe

Hydraulic digging

The sections of the arm of a digger are moved by powerful hydraulic rams, each with a cylinder and piston. Hydraulic fluid is pumped to the cylinders by a pump powered by the digger's diesel engine. The fluid flows along very strong pipes called hydraulic lines, which you can see on the upper part of the arm.

Pumping water

Moving a water pump's piston in and out moves water from the pipe on the left to the pipe on the right. The valve opens to let water through as the piston moves in. The valve shuts automatically as the piston moves out because the water presses the valve closed.

Breaking through

A pneumatic drill is an air-powered drill used to break up road surfaces and concrete. The air forces the drill's heavy blade to jump up and down very quickly. The drill needs a supply of compressed air to make it work, which comes along a strong, rubber pipe from a machine called a compressor.

LIQUID AND AIR AT WORK

MAKE AN HYDRAULIC LIFTER

You will need: *large plastic bottle, scissors, airtight plastic bag, plastic tubing, sticky tape, plastic funnel, spray can lid, heavy weight, jug of water.*

Hydraulic machinery uses a liquid to transmit power, while pneumatic machinery uses compressed air. The first project shows you how to make a simple hydraulic machine that uses water pressure to lift an object upwards. A central reservoir (a jug of water) is poured into a pipe. The water fills up a plastic bag, which is forced to expand in a narrow cylinder. This forces up a platform, which in turn raises a heavy object. Many cranes, excavators and trucks use this principle to lift heavy loads, using hydraulic rams.

The second project shows you how to make a simple air pump. An air pump works by sucking air in one hole and pushing it out of another. A valve stops the air being sucked in and pushed out of the wrong holes. When the air tries to flow through one way, the valve opens, but when the air tries to flow through the other way the valve stays shut.

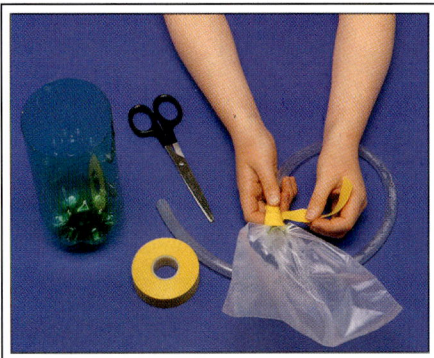

1 Cut the top off the large plastic bottle. Make sure the plastic bag is airtight and wrap its neck over the end of a length of plastic tubing. Seal the bag to the tube with tape.

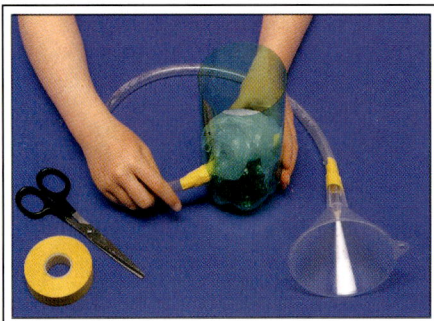

Firing water
Fire-fighters spray water on to fires through hoses so that they can stand back from the flames. The water is pumped along the hoses by a powerful pump on the fire engine.

2 Fix a funnel to the other end of the tube. Make a hole at the base of the bottle and feed the bag and tubing through. The bag should sit in the bottom of the bottle.

3 Put the spray can lid on top of the bag and rest a book, or another heavy object, on top of the bottle. Lift the funnel end of the tubing up, and slowly pour in water. What happens to the can lid and the book?

MAKE AN AIR PUMP

You will need: *large plastic bottle, scissors, hammer, small nails, wooden stick or dowelling, card, sticky tape, table tennis ball.*

1 Cut around the large plastic bottle, about one third up from the bottom. Cut a slit down the side of the bottom part of the bottle so that it will slide inside the top part.

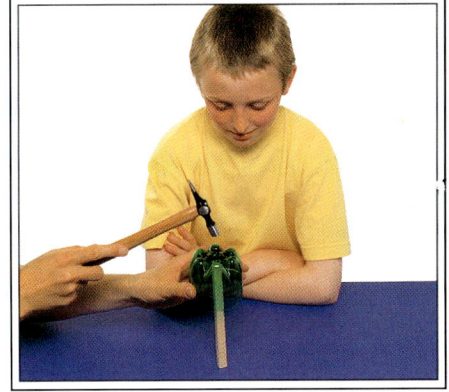

2 Ask an adult to help you nail the bottom of the bottle to the end of a wooden stick or piece of dowelling. You have now made a piston for your air pump.

3 Cut a hole about 1 cm across near the neck of the bottle. Cut a piece of card about 2cm x 2cm. Tape one edge of the card to the bottle to form a flap over the hole.

4 Drop a table tennis ball into the top part of the bottle so that it rests in the neck. Push the bottom part of the bottle (the piston) into the top part (the cylinder).

FACT BOX

• A fire-engine pump can pump 1,000 litres of water a minute – enough to fill eight large fizzy drink bottles a second.

• Fire-fighters free people trapped in crashed cars with hydraulically powered cutting and spreading machines.

5 Move the piston in and out to suck air into the bottle and out of the hole. Can you see how both the valves work? The flap should automatically close when you pull the piston out.

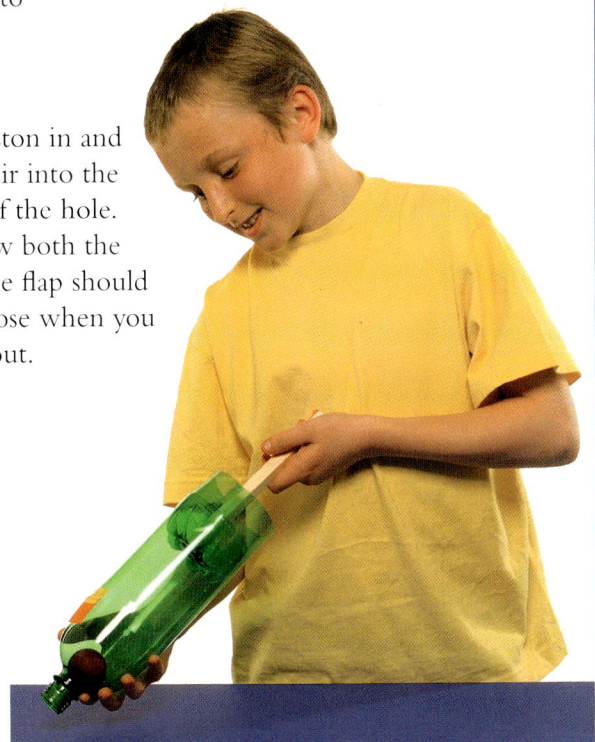

Skip-lifting truck
A skip truck has hydraulic rams to lift a full skip. The rams are controlled by levers near the cab, and powered by a pump operated by the engine.

MACHINES AT HOME

Your home is full of machines. Look in the kitchen, the bathroom, the living room and bedroom. In your kitchen you should find several simple gadgets, such as can-openers, taps, scissors and bottle openers. There might also be more complicated machines, such as a washing machine or a dishwasher. Other machines you might find include a vacuum cleaner and a refrigerator. In other rooms there may be a hairdryer, a shower and a television. Even the zips on your clothes are machines. Think about how each one might save you time and effort. What would life be like without them?

Most machines not only save you work, but also improve the results – a modern washing machine cleans clothes better than an old-fashioned tub and a vacuum cleaner is more efficient than a broom. Many machines save time, too. For example, it is far quicker to heat food in a microwave oven than over an open fire. Many of these machines need electricity to work and are powered from the mains supply.

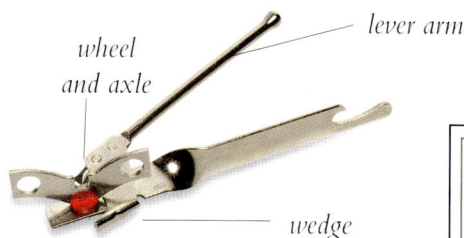

zip fastener

Zip it up

One of the simplest machines is the zip. If you look carefully at the zip fastener, you will see a wedge shape in the middle. This forces the two edges of the zip together to do it up, and apart again to undo it. Before there were zips, people had to do their clothes up with buttons or hooks and eyes, which took longer.

wheel and axle

lever arm

wedge

Can-opener

Can you see four different types of machine in a can opener? You should be able to find levers, a wedge, a wheel and axle and a gear wheel. Together, they make it simple to open a can.

FACT BOX

• The zip was invented in 1893. The first zips were unreliable until tiny bumps and hollows were added to the end of each tooth, to help the teeth interlock.

• Electrically powered domestic machines were only possible once mains electricity was developed in the 1880s.

• One of the earliest vacuum cleaners was built in England, in 1901. It was so large that it had to be pulled by a horse and powered by a petrol engine!

• The spin dryer was thought of by a French engineer in 1865, but it was not developed until the 1920s.

What, no bag?

This clever bagless cleaner spins the dusty air at high speed, which throws the dust to the sides of the dust-collecting container. Most vacuum cleaners have a bag that lets air through but traps dust, and the bag has to be replaced regularly. The bagless cleaner's container lasts for much longer.

How a fridge works

Inside a refrigerator is a pump that squeezes a special liquid called a refrigerant. As the refrigerant expands again, it uses up heat, making the compartment cold.

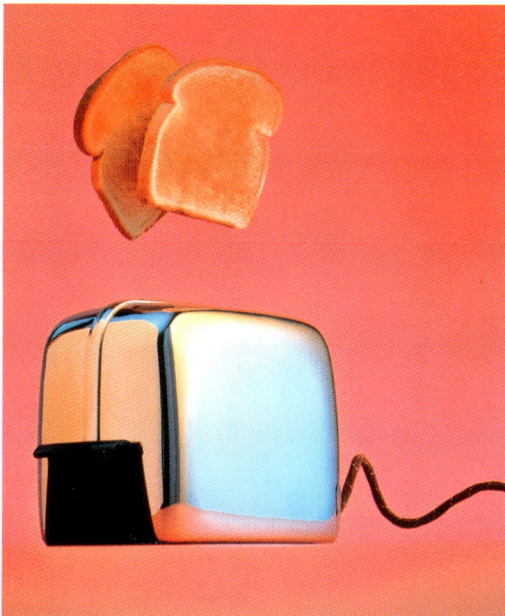

Washing by machine

A modern washing machine is a combination of several machines. It has electric motors (to turn the drum), pumps (to pump water in and out) and valves (that let water in or out). All these machines are controlled by an automatic programme timer.

Hairdryer

Small, mains-powered electric motors make it possible to make compact machines such as hairdryers. The motor in a hairdryer works a fan. This blows air across a coil of wire that is heated instantly by electricity, making the air warm.

Perfect toast

A toaster is a machine that heats bread using electric heating elements until it detects that the surface of the bread is hot enough. Then it ejects the toast and turns off the elements.

TRANSPORT MACHINES

Bicycles, cars, buses, trucks, trains, ships and aircraft are all machines used for transport. They all make it easier and quicker to travel from one place to another by making wide use of different types of engines, motors, gears and wheels. The bicycle is one of the most complicated machines that relies on human muscle power to work. A bicycle includes several types of simple machine, such as wheels, axles and levers, and is designed to reduce effort to a minimum.

Larger transport machines have engines and motors to power them. Many also make use of hydraulic, pneumatic and electronic systems. The different systems combine to make the machine efficient, so that it uses the minimum amount of fuel or electricity, and safe, so that there is a low risk of accidents, and passengers are well protected.

Hopalong hobbyhorse
The first bicycles had no gears and no pedals. They were called hobbyhorses and the riders had to push them along the ground with their feet. They were still quicker than walking.

On your bicycle
A cyclist uses her energy to push down on the pedals. The gear system uses this push to turn the back wheel and drive the bike forwards. The tyres rub against the road, causing friction, a force that slows things down. Air hitting her body, and her weight, cause her to slow down, too.

The gear system allows a cyclist to travel quickly or slowly and still pedal at a comfortable rate.

The brake lever on the handlebar pulls a cable that makes a brake block press on the wheel rim.

A smooth ride
A pump is used to pump air into the tyres. A valve in the tyre lets air in, but stops it escaping. Tyres are pumped full of air to give a smoother, easier ride.

Electric trains

Overhead cables suspended above the track provide the power for the electric motors that move fast express trains, such as this Swedish X2000. Electric motors work well at low speed and high speed, so no complicated gears are needed for the train to speed up or slow down. Inside the locomotive cars at each end of the train are electric circuits that control the flow of electricity to the motors. The driver controls the speed of the train from the cab at the front. The train is also streamlined (shaped to move smoothly) so that it cuts easily through the air.

Car parts

All modern cars, from sports cars to small family cars, have similar parts. They are moved by an internal-combustion engine (at the front) which burns petrol or diesel fuel stored in a tank (at the rear). All the parts are attached to a steel body shell.

Aircraft parts

The flaps that extend from an aircraft's wings to provide extra lift during take-off and landing are controlled by hydraulic systems. Airliners, such as this Airbus A340, are the most complex transport machines of all, with thousands of parts. They are moved through the air by powerful jet engines, which are complex machines themselves. Safety is very important, so most of the aircraft's systems have back-up systems in case they go wrong.

BUILDING MACHINES

Constructing houses, office blocks, bridges, roads and railways involves digging into the ground, moving rock and earth, and transporting and lifting steel, concrete and other heavy building materials. There are specialized construction machines, such as diggers, bulldozers, concrete mixers and cranes, to carry out all these jobs. Many of them use the principles of simple machines to work. For example, cranes use pulleys and balanced levers to help them lift. Most construction machines have large diesel engines to provide the power they need, and some have hydraulic or pneumatic systems to move their parts.

Machinery of old
The Flemish artist Pieter Brueghel painted the mythical Tower of Babel in 1563. It shows the sort of construction machines that were in use in the 1500s, such as chisels, levers, pulleys and simple cranes, operated by large treadmills. The huge cathedrals found in many European cities were built with simple machines like these.

FACT BOX

• The height of a tower crane's tower can be increased. A new section of tower is hauled up and positioned on top of the existing tower.

• Tunnels that go through soft rock, such as chalk, are dug with tunnel boring machines. The machine bores its way through the rock with a rotating cutting head.

• Around 2,000 years ago the Romans used cranes for building. The cranes were powered by slaves walking round in a giant treadmill.

Earth mover
A bulldozer is used to push rock, soil and rubble away to clear a building site ready for work to start. Its wide tracks, called caterpillar tracks, stop it sinking into muddy ground.

Digging out
A mechanical excavator is used to dig up rock and soil. It makes trenches for pipes, and holes for foundations. Its powerful digging arm is operated by hydraulic rams.

Loading machine

A machine called a loader has a wide bucket that skims along the ground scooping up waste soil. When the bucket is full, hydraulic rams lift it into the air so that the loader can carry it to a waiting dumper truck.

Mixing it up

A concrete mixer carries concrete to the building site from the factory. Inside the drum a blade, like a screw thread, mixes the concrete. The blade stays still while the drum rotates.

Hammering in

A pile driver hammers piles, or metal posts, into the ground. It repeatedly lifts a large weight with its crane and drops it on to the top of the pile. The piles form the foundation of a new building.

Tipping out

Dumper trucks are used to deliver hardcore (crushed up stones used for foundations) and to take away unwanted soil. To empty the load on to the ground, the back of the dumper is tipped up by hydraulic rams. The load slides to the ground.

Towering crane

These tower cranes look flimsy, but they do not topple over even when they are lifting heavy weights. This is because of a concrete counterweight behind the cab.

ON THE FARM

Some of the oldest types of machines in the world are used for agriculture. Farmers use machines to prepare the soil, to sow and harvest their crops, and to feed and milk their animals. One of the first, and still one of the most important farm machines, was the plough. Archaeologists have found evidence of ploughs from about 9,000 years ago. They began as a simple, sharpened stick that was used to turn up the soil. Today, a seven-furrow plough hauled behind a modern tractor can cover 40 hectares of land – as much as 80 football pitches – in a day.

Modern farming uses many specialized machines to make cultivated land more productive. In some parts of the world, powered machinery, usually operated by a tractor, does all the work. But in many countries, ploughs are pulled by animals, and crops are harvested using simple hand tools.

Tractor and plough
Modern, tractor-pulled ploughs have several individual ploughs in a row to break up the soil into furrows. This makes it much quicker to plough a field than with a single plough. At the rear end of the tractor is a rotating shaft called a take-off shaft. It provides the power for the plough.

FACT BOX

• On many farms in arid areas, the pumps used to raise water from wells or streams for irrigation, and for animals to drink, are powered by small windmills.

• One of the most important agricultural inventions was the seed drill, which planted seeds in neat rows and at the correct depth. It was invented more than five thousand years ago.

Steam power
Steam-driven traction engines were the first type of tractor. This one was built in 1880. It replaced the farm's horses and powered other machines, such as the thresher shown here.

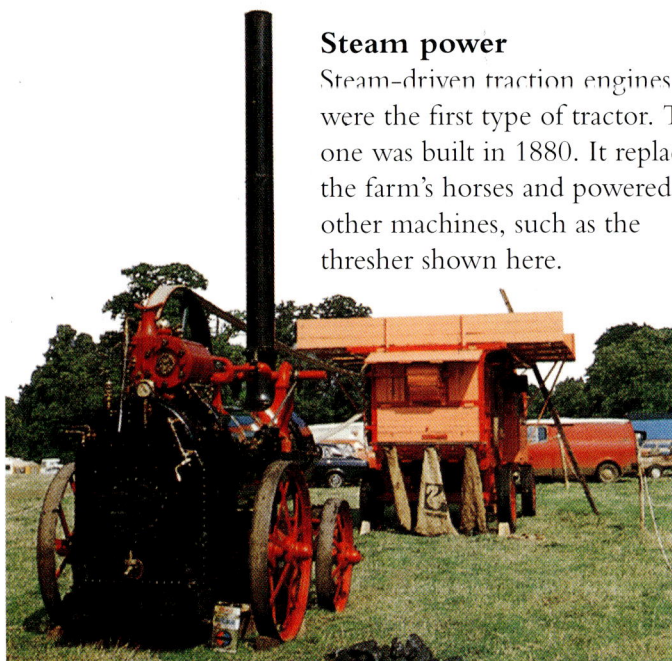

Animal power
A water buffalo pulls a plough through the soil. Animals, especially oxen, are still widely used by farmers who cannot afford machinery or who live in hilly or mountainous areas.

Pneumatic milking

In a milking parlour, milk is sucked from cows' udders by pneumatic milking machines. A large parlour can milk dozens of cows at the same time. The milk pours into tanks, where it is measured and then pumped to a refrigerated tank to wait for collection by a milk tanker.

Hay wrapper

A baling machine automatically makes hay into bales and wraps them in plastic to keep them dry. Here, the machine is spinning the bale one way as it wraps plastic sheeting around it the other way.

Combine harvester

A combine harvester cuts and collects crops. A reel sweeps the crop into a cutter bar that slices the stalks off at ground level. The stalks are pushed into the machine and grain is stripped from them. Special screws, called impeller screws or augers, are often used to move the grain around inside the harvester.

A close shave

A sheep farmer uses electrically operated shears to cut the fleece from a sheep. The shears work like a pair of scissors. The electric motor moves the blades together and apart at high speed.

MAKING FARM MACHINES

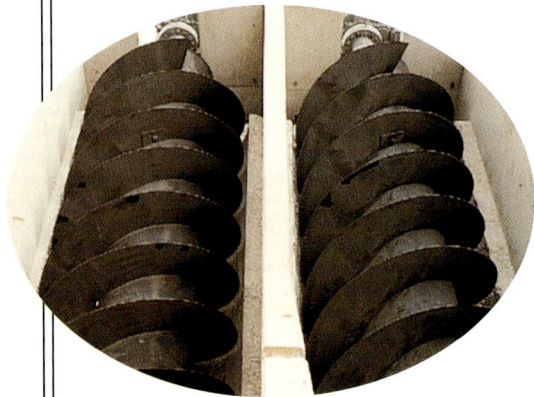

The two projects on these pages will show you how to make two simple machines like those used on farms. The first is an Archimedean screw. In parts of the world where water pumps are expensive to buy and run, Archimedean screws are used to move water uphill in order to irrigate crops. The machine is made up of a large screw inside a pipe. One end of the machine is placed in the water and, as a handle is turned, the screw inside revolves, carrying water upwards. This water-lifting device has been in use for centuries and it is named after the ancient Greek scientist, Archimedes.

The second project is to make a simple plough. By pushing the plough through a tray of damp sand you will be able to see how the special, curved, wedge shape of a real plough lifts and turns the soil to make a furrow. A furrow is a trench in which the farmer plants the seeds.

Screwed-up water
Inside an Archimedean screw is a wide screw thread. Water is trapped in the thread and is forced to move upwards as the screw is turned. A screw thread like this is also called an auger.

MAKE AN ARCHIMEDEAN SCREW

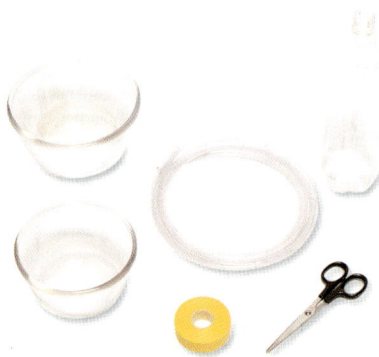

You will need:
small plastic bottle, scissors, plastic tubing, waterproof sticky tape, two bowls.

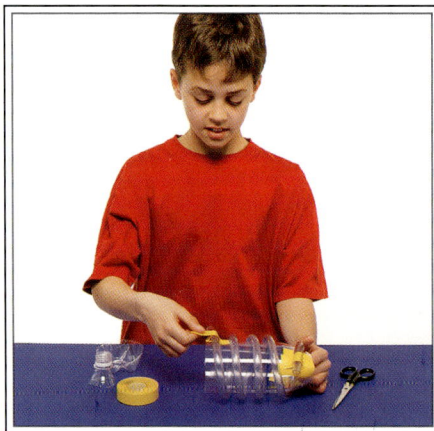

1 Cut the top and bottom off the bottle. Wrap a length of plastic tubing around the bottle to make a screw thread shape. Tape the tubing in place with waterproof sticky tape.

2 Put one end of the bottle in a bowl of water and rest it on the bowl's edge. Place the other bowl at the end of the tubing. Slowly turn the bottle. After a few turns, the water will pour out of the top of the tubing.

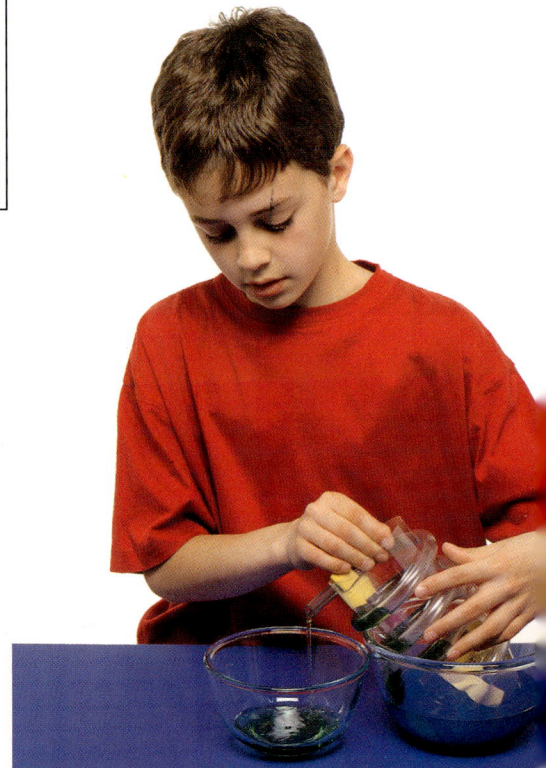

FACT BOX

• Every year Australian farmers have to shear tens of millions of sheep. As an experiment in 1986, Australian engineers built a robot that could shear a sheep in about 90 seconds.

• The first ploughs were made from wood or from stag antlers. They were invented in Egypt and India about 5,500 years ago.

MAKE A SIMPLE PLOUGH

You will need:
small plastic bottle, scissors, strip of wood or dowelling, drawing pin, tray of damp sand.

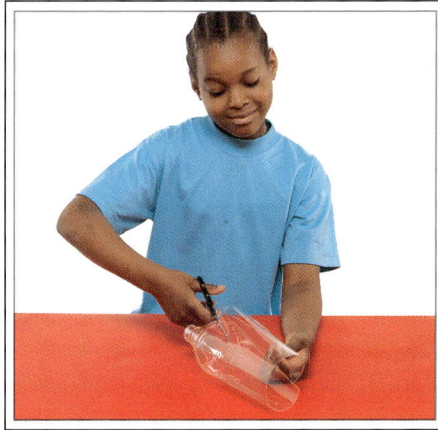

1 Start by cutting a triangle of plastic from one side of the small plastic drinks bottle. This triangle will form the blade of your plough.

2 Cut a slot in the triangle, as shown above. Fold the triangle in half along the line of the slot against the curve of the plastic.

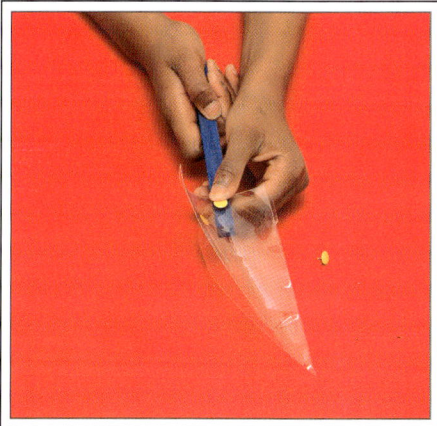

Soil-turning wedges
Each metal blade on this plough works as a wedge. The front point slices easily through the soil, splitting it up. As the soil slides along the blade's side, the curved shape lifts and turns it over. The plough buries weeds and brings fresh soil to the surface for new crops to grow in. This is called tilling.

3 Holding the two sides of the blade together, fix it to the length of wood or dowelling with a drawing pin. Make sure the blade is securely attached to the handle.

4 Fill up the tray with damp sand and push the plough through the sand in lines. Does your plough lift and turn the soil to make a furrow?

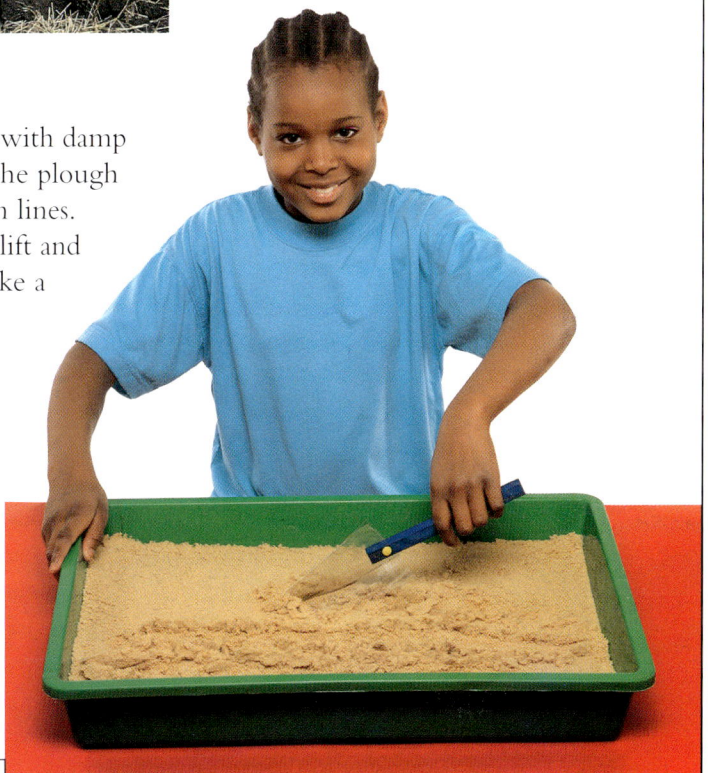

Guided plough
The wheels on a plough from the 1400s stop it from sinking too far into the ground. The farmer guides the plough to make a neat furrow, while a helper urges on oxen and horses.

ELECTRONIC MACHINES

Most of the machines we use have moving parts that are operated by hand or by an engine or motor. These devices are called mechanical machines. Many modern machines, however, such as computers, have no moving parts. They are called electronic machines. Inside an electronic machine lots of components are connected together to form a continuous wire, called a circuit, around which an electric current flows. The components control the way electricity flows around the circuits and so control what the machine does. Complicated electronic circuits, containing hundreds of thousands of components, can be contained on a single microchip a few millimetres across.

Some electronic machines, such as weighing scales and digital watches, do the same job as mechanical machines. Many modern machines, such as robots, are combinations of mechanical and electronic parts.

Weighing scale
When an orange is put on a scale, it presses on an electronic device called a strain gauge. The gauge controls the strength of a tiny electric current. Electronics inside the machine detect the size of the current, work out the orange's weight, and show it on a display panel to be read.

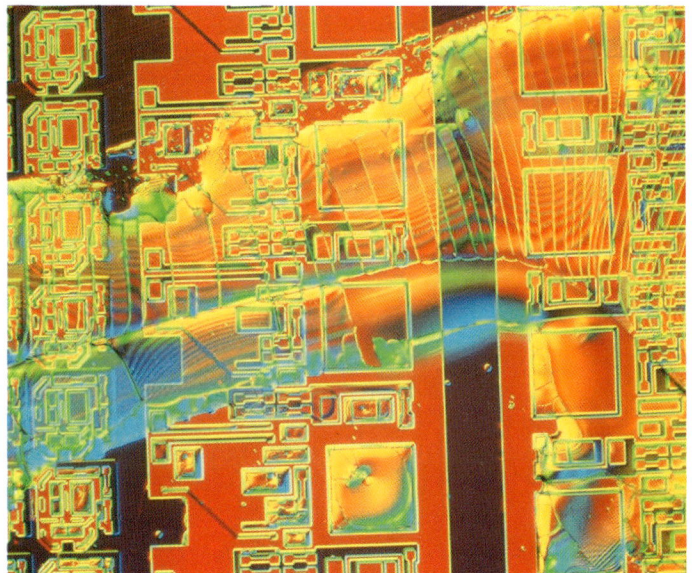

Internet on the phone
A mobile phone is an extremely complex machine in a tiny case. It is a combination of a telephone and radio receiver and transmitter. As well as being a phone, this machine can send and receive e-mails, and download web pages from the Internet and display them on its screen.

Palm-top computer
The personal digital assistant (PDA) is a small but powerful type of electronic machine. It is a palm-sized computer that stores personal data.

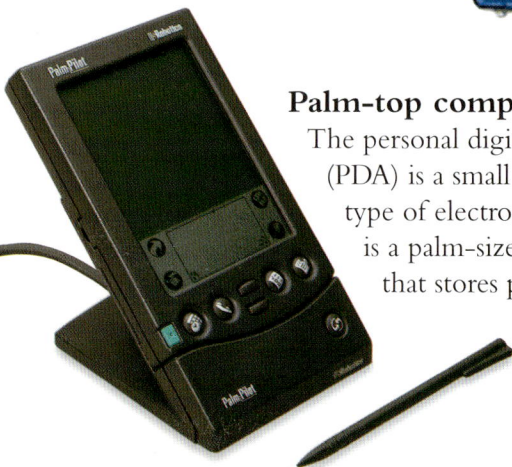

Microscopic microchips
A photomicrograph (a photograph taken through a microscope) shows the tiny components on a microchip, each too small to see with the naked eye. The chip starts as a thin layer of silicon, and the components are built up using complex chemical and photographic processes.

The first computers

One of the first electronic computers was called ENIAC (Electronic Numerical Integrator And Calculator). It was built in the 1940s. It took up a huge amount of space because its electronic parts were thousands of times bigger than today's microchips. ENIAC needed several rooms to fit in all its valves, wires and dials, but it was less powerful than a modern pocket calculator.

Inside a computer system

A computer is an extremely complicated machine, but the way it works is quite easy to understand if you think of it in several parts. Each part does its own job, such as storing or sending information.

display shows words and pictures

memory stores data and programs

central processing unit acts like the computer's brain

input and output receive and send data

MEM

CPU

IN AND OUT

disk drives store data and programs

CD-ROM drive stores data and programs

bus moves data from one part of the computer to another

modem connects the computer to the telephone system

mouse clicks on areas of the display

Information is inputted through the keyboard

FACT BOX

• In the 1830s, British scientist Charles Babbage designed a mechanical calculator called an Analytical Engine. Unfortunately, although it would have worked, it was never made because its parts were too complex.

• The first PC (personal computer) went on sale in 1975. It had 256 bytes of memory. PCs today have around 128 megabytes of memory – or more than 128 million bytes.

• The fastest supercomputers can add together more than a quarter of a million million numbers in a second.

MACHINES IN INDUSTRY

In a spin
A steam-powered circular saw is used to cut large logs into shape. The saw has a razor-sharp blade with teeth that cut into the material as it spins. The object that is being cut is moved backwards or forwards across the blade.

Machine tools are machines used in factories to manufacture objects. The operations they are used for are cutting, drilling, grinding, turning and milling. Each of these operations is done by a special machine. For example, the operation of turning (forming a curve in the material) is done on a lathe, and cutting is done with a saw. All machine tools have a cutting blade or edge, which is normally made of metal, but may include diamond or other tough materials. The blade moves against the object being cut, called the workpiece, shaving off unwanted material.

Machine tools are used to make engine parts and other complex machines in which the parts have to fit together perfectly. Industrial robots are versatile machines that can be programmed to do many jobs, such as moving workpieces or drilling very accurately.

A perfect fit
Under computer control, this miniature milling machine is shaping a piece of ceramic material so that it will fit perfectly into a cavity in a dental patient's tooth. A milling machine cuts away areas of a piece of material. The cutting tool has rotating teeth, similar to a gear wheel.

Pedal power
A pole lathe is powered by a foot-operated pedal. The lathe spins the workpiece around very fast. The operator presses cutting tools against the spinning wood, shaving away a layer each time. How accurately the workpiece is finished depends on the skill of the lathe operator.

Pressed panels
A machine called a die press flattens sheets of steel into shaped panels, such as those used for car bonnets. The top part of the machine moves down to press the panel into shape. Each sheet of steel is pressed into exactly the same shape every time.

Digital control

An engineer makes a heating element from a graphite rod using a computer-controlled milling machine. Data describing the shape and size of the heating element is fed into the machine's computer, normally from another computer on which it has been designed. The computer then works out the cutting movements required to make the heating element from the rod, and operates the milling machine very precisely.

Keeping cool

The milky liquid pouring on to this drill is, in fact, coloured water. As the drill bit cuts into the metal workpiece, it gets very hot. The water keeps the drill cool, stopping the tool melting and washing waste metal away.

Industrial robots

Robots are used for welding car components together. The robot is shown how to do the job once and can then do it over and over again much faster than a human worker.

FACT BOX

• In some industries, high-energy lasers are used for cutting and shaping materials instead of traditional machine tools. The most powerful lasers can cut through 6cm of steel.

• In some car-making factories, parts for the cars are delivered by robot vehicles that are programmed to drive themselves around the floor of the factory.

MACHINES OF THE FUTURE

Machines that do complicated jobs need controls. Some of these machines need a human operator who controls the machine manually. For example, a car needs a driver to control its speed and direction. Other machines control themselves – once they are turned on, they do their job automatically. For example, an automatic washing machine washes and spins your clothes at the press of a button. One of the first machines to use a form of automatic control was the Jacquard loom, which wove material. Punched paper cards were fed into the loom and told it which threads were to be used. Today, many machines are controlled by computer to perform a set task whenever it is required. The most advanced machines are even able to check their own work and change it if necessary.

Flying by wires
Airliners and fighter aircraft may have a "fly-by-wire" control system, where a computer, rather than the pilot, actually flies the plane. The pilot monitors how the plane is working by watching a computer screen instead of dials.

Journey through space
Shuttle-like space planes, such as the experimental X 33, will eventually be used to transport passengers via space. Space planes could reduce the usual flight time from New York to Tokyo from nearly 14 hours to just a couple of hours.

Robotic rover
A toy robot dog has built-in artificial intelligence. It knows nothing at first, but it gradually works out the layout of its new home and learns to respond to its new owner's commands.

Tiny machine
The rotor in this photograph is actually only about 0.5mm across. It is part of a meter that measures liquid flow. It is made of silicon and was manufactured using similar methods to those used to make microchips. Tiny machines such as this are called micromachines.

Robotic surgeon

In the future, it is possible that microscopic machines will be used in surgery. In this futuristic painting a microscopic robot is repairing a human body. The robot, just 0.1mm long, has been injected into a blood vessel through the needle on the right. Around the robot are red blood cells. With its rotating blades, the robot is cutting away a blockage made of debris (shown in grey). The robot sucks up the debris for removal.

Invisible gears

These gear wheels look quite ordinary, but they were made using microscopic experimental technology called nanotechnology. The width of the wheels is less than the width of a human hair. A hundred of these gear wheels piled up would be only as tall as the thickness of a sheet of paper!

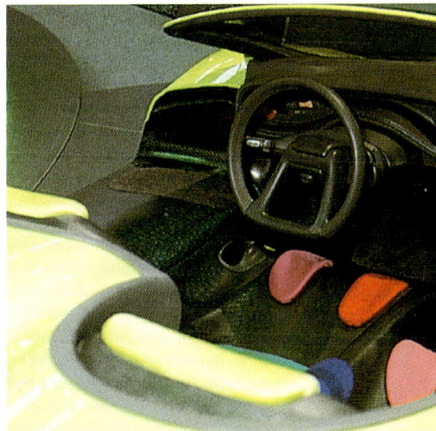

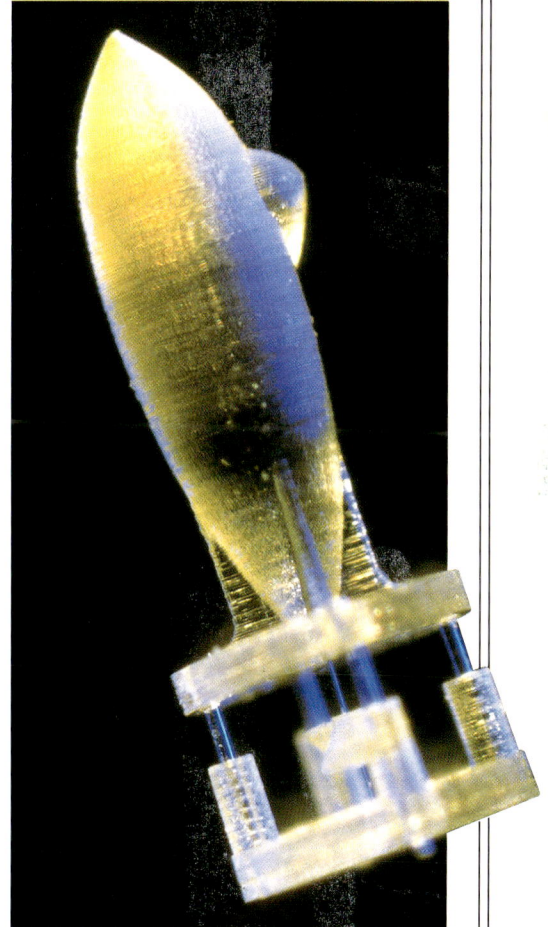

Handy android

An android (a human-like robot) uses electronic eyes and ears to work out where objects are, and its hand to pick them up. With its artificial intelligence, it can decide what sort of object it is holding. Androids help scientists to research how robots can be made to act like humans.

Car control

Many of this car's systems are controlled by a microchip called a microprocessor. It continually checks signals from sensors and sends a control signal back again. It calculates the speed, distance and fuel consumption of the car and displays them on the dashboard.

Mini submarine

A miniature submarine that measures just 4mm from top to bottom was made using an experimental technique for creating microscopic machine parts. The technique uses tiny laser beams to solidify selected parts of a pool of liquid plastic to form the submarine's shape.

AUTOMATIC CONTROL

CONTROLLING A ROBOT

You will need:
blindfold, egg and egg-cup.

1 Ask a friend to put on the blindfold. Use the list of commands opposite to direct your friend to where the egg is located.

2 Your friend should not know where the egg is or what to do with it. Instruct your friend to carefully pick the egg up. Only use commands in the list.

Machines that perform very difficult, complicated tasks need to be controlled with precision. Robots are machines that are programmed with instructions for different situations. They can respond to each situation in an 'intelligent' way, rather like human beings. However, although robots seem to be very clever, they can only do what they are told to do. The project below will show you how tricky it is to programme a robot to do even the simplest job. Using only the words that are from the list of commands, see if a friend can carry out the task successfully.

The second project shows you how to make a simple control disc. This is the sort of device used to control some washing machines. The metal track on the disc is part of an electric circuit. As the disc turns, the track completes or breaks the circuit, turning parts of the machine, such as lights and motors, on and off.

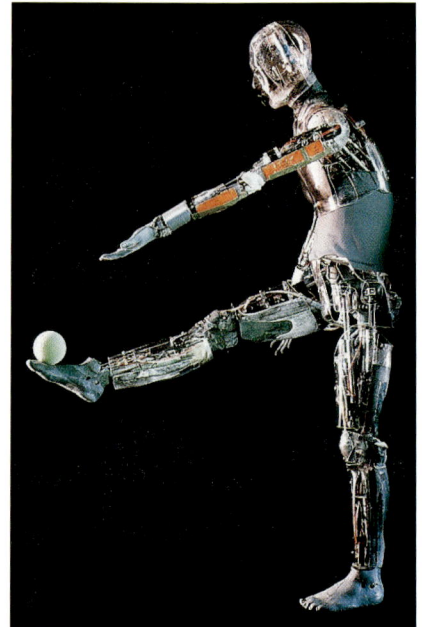

Robot commands

FORWARD
STOP
TURN LEFT
TURN RIGHT
ARM UP
ARM DOWN
CLOSE FINGERS
OPEN FINGERS

3 Now ask your friend to accurately place the egg on another surface. See if your friend can put it in the egg-cup. How quickly was your friend able to complete the task? The faster your friend completes the task, the better you are at programming.

MAKE A CONTROL DISC

You will need: *pair of compasses and pencil, ruler, card, scissors, aluminium foil dish, glue, sticky tape, paper fastener, wire, three plastic-coated wires, battery, torch bulb and holder.*

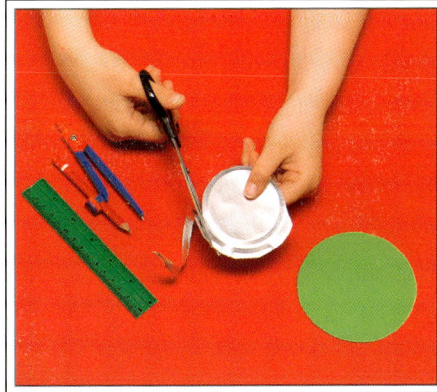

1 Use a compass to mark out a 10cm disc on the card and cut it out. Also cut a 6cm ring from the foil dish and glue it on to the card.

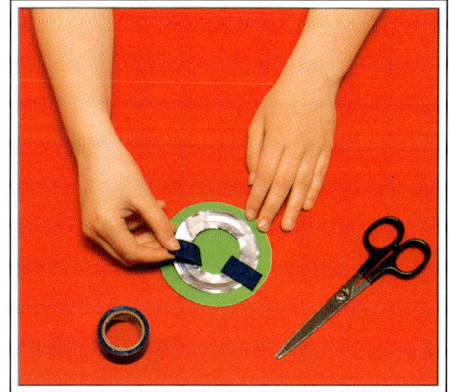

2 Put pieces of sticky tape across the foil track. The bare foil will complete the circuit. The pieces of sticky tape will break the circuit.

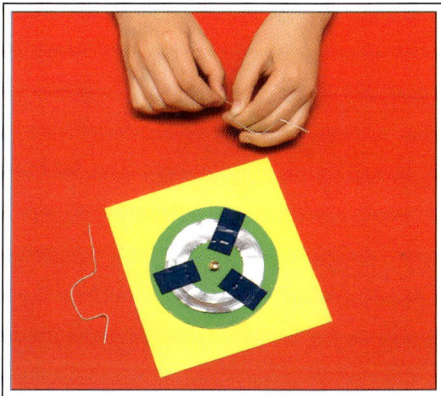

3 Push a paper fastener through the middle of the disc and mount it on to a piece of card. Using the wire, make two contacts with a bend in the middle, as shown.

Loom control

The Jacquard loom, invented in 1801, was one of the first machines with automatic control. Cards with patterns of holes in them, called punched cards, controlled how threads were woven together to create patterns in the fabric that the loom made. The pattern created could be changed simply by changing to another set of cards with a different pattern of holes.

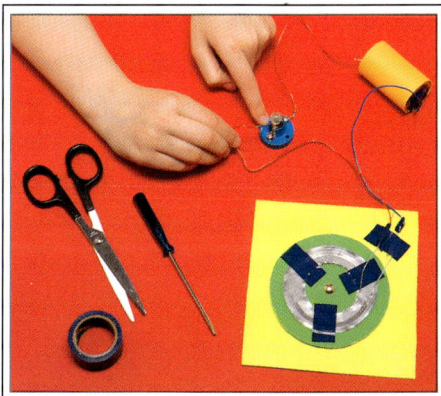

4 Stick the contacts to the card so they press on the foil. Connect a battery to a bulb with plastic-coated wire. Attach a second piece of plastic-coated wire to the bulb, and a third to the battery.

5 Attach the two loose wires to the two contacts on the card. You have now made a circuit. Turn the disc slowly. The light bulb goes on and off as the disc turns. As the contacts go over a piece of sticky tape, the circuit is broken and the light goes out. When they touch the foil again, the circuit is completed and the light comes back on.

GLOSSARY

A

acupuncture
An ancient form of Chinese medicine in which special needles are inserted into a patient's body to cure illness.

artificial
Not achieved by natural means.

astrology
The belief that human lives are affected by the ways in which the planets and stars behave.

auger
A large tool shaped like a corkscrew, for boring holes in the ground.

axe
A wedge of metal on the end of a long handle, which is used to split wood.

axle
A bar which joins wheels together. Axles turn on bearings.

B

banner
Any flag-like design that represents a person's or a country's importance.

belt drive
A device that uses a belt to transfer a drive from one pulley to another. Many sewing machines have belt drives.

bevelled gears
Gears with teeth set at an angle. These gears are usually set at right angles to each other and change the direction of the drive.

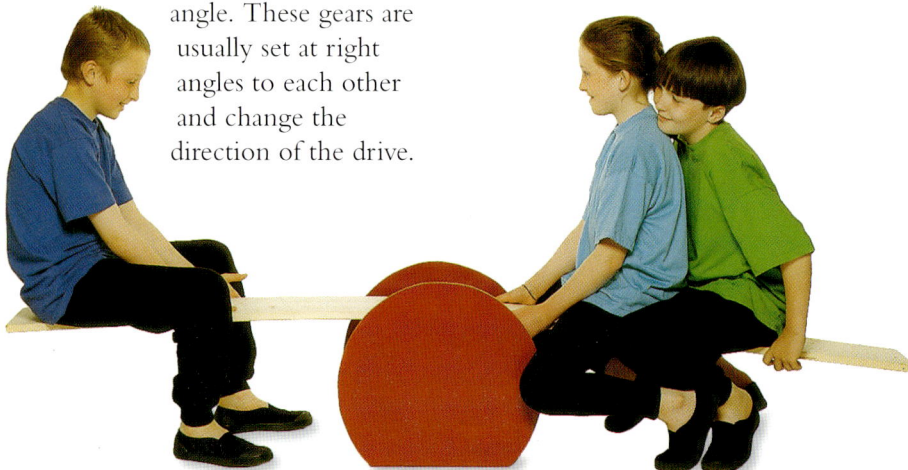

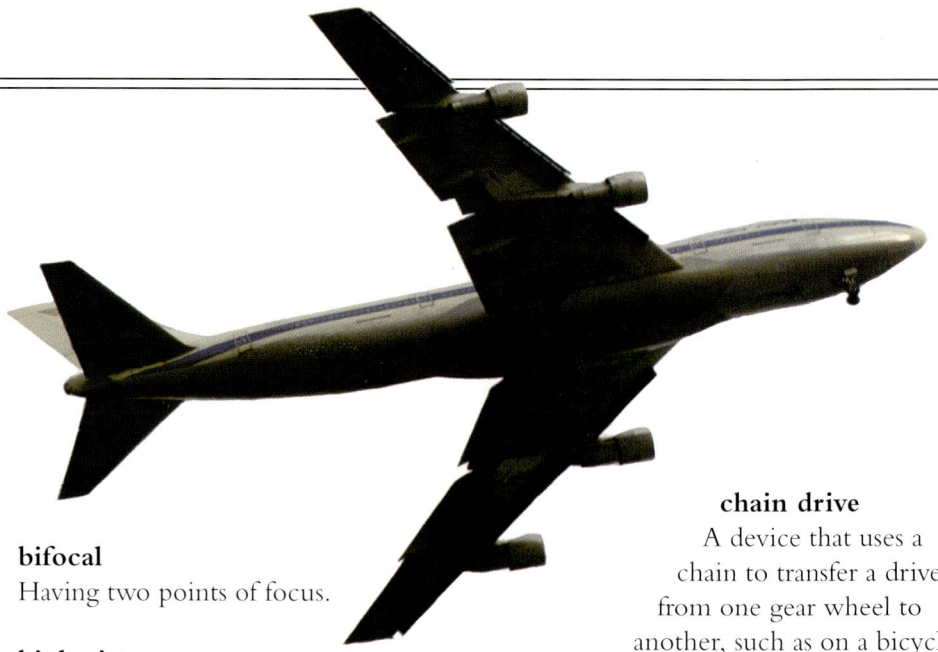

bifocal
Having two points of focus.

biologist
A scientist who investigates the ways in which living things grow and how they are made.

bionic machine
A machine that acts like a living thing.

block and tackle
A device that uses two sets of pulley blocks to help raise very heavy weights.

C

capstan wheel
A revolving barrel in which the effort is applied by pushing against long horizontal levers. Capstans were used to raise anchors on ships.

carbon dioxide
A naturally occurring gas present everywhere in the air people breathe.

cellular
Things built out of single units joined together to make a whole.

chain drive
A device that uses a chain to transfer a drive from one gear wheel to another, such as on a bicycle.

chemical
A pure substance present in the Earth that can be formed by or react to other substances.

chisel
A metal cutting tool with a wedge at its edge.

cholera
A dangerous illness caused by drinking water that is polluted with human waste.

compressed air
Air that has been squashed into a smaller volume than usual.

construction machine
A machine, such as a digger, that is used on building sites.

cotton
Cloth woven from the soft material produced by the cotton plant.

crankshaft
An axle that has parts of it bent at right angles so that the up and down motion of pistons is turned into circular motion.

D

data
Any collection of information that is collected for the purpose of putting it into a pattern.

die press
A machine that squeezes metal into a shape using great force.

disinfectant
A substance that kills germs.

draughtsman
A person who makes drawings for specific purposes such as building a new house.

drill
A cutting tool that has a spiral blade for removing waste material.

driveshaft
The bar that is turned by an engine to drive wheels.

drug
A substance used for fighting illness. Some drugs are poisonous if not taken under the care of a medically qualified person.

E

effort
The force applied to a lever or other simple machine to move a load.

electricity
The form of energy produced by the movement of electrons (charged particles) in atoms.

electron
A tiny part of an atom that has an electric charge.

electronic circuit
A circuit that consists of transistors.

e-mail
A method of communication between computers.

engine
A device that provides turning power.

F

fax
A document that can contain both words and pictures sent from one person to another along a telephone line.

fax machine
A machine that can both send and receive words and pictures that have been changed into electrical messages.

first class lever
A simple lever such as a see-saw, in which the pivot is between the two ends.

fleece
The coat hair of animals such as sheep and goats that is spun into yarn and woven into cloth.

force
A push or a pull which results in an object moving faster or slower.

fungus
A plant-like growth such as mushrooms, toadstools and mould.

G

gear
A wheel that has teeth that mesh with another gearwheel's teeth.

gearbox
A set of gearwheels of different sizes that can turn wheels at different speeds and with different mechanical advantages.

germ
A kind of micro-organism that, once it is inside the human body, can cause illness.

gravity
The pulling force that operates between all masses.

groove
A channel cut in a pulley wheel to keep a belt drive in place.

H

hertz
The name for the frequency of an electromagnetic wave.

hydraulics
The use of water or other liquids to move pistons and other devices.

hydroelectric power
Power derived from moving water.

I

inclined plane
A slope up which heavy objects can be moved more easily than by raising them vertically.

infection
An attack on the cells in the body by germs that causes people to fall ill.

internal-combustion engine
A motor that burns petrol or diesel in cylinders to supply hot gases to push pistons.

inventor
A person who finds a new way to make human knowledge useful in people's everyday lives.

K

keystone
The central stone in the arch of a bridge or curved part of a building.

L

laboratory
The workroom of a scientist where new ideas are carried out in the form of experiments.

laser
A device which produces an intense beam of light.

lathe
A machine that spins an object against a cutting tool.

lens
A curved piece of glass that, when people look through it, makes objects look bigger.

lever
A long bar that is used against a pivot to help move a heavy object.

load
The weight moved by a lever or other machine.

lock
A device to prevent something, such as a door, from opening.

loom
A machine made for the purpose of weaving thread into fabric.

M

magnet
A piece of iron or other material that attracts other pieces of iron.

mains power
Electricity supplied to homes from power stations.

malaria
A deadly disease carried by mosquitoes, mainly in tropical and sub-tropical parts of the world.

mass
The amount of material in an object. Mass is measured in kilograms.

mechanical advantage
The number of times by which the load is greater than the effort.

medieval
Describing anything from the period in human history between about AD1000 and 1500.

microchip
A device that has thousands of electronic circuits on one sliver of silicon.

micromachine
A very small machine.

microwaves
Radio waves that are most often used today to cook food quickly in microwave ovens.

mill
To grind or cut metal, stone or wood using a machine with a turning motion.

mortar
A mixture, usually of sand, cement and water, used to fix bricks or blocks of stone firmly together.

mould
A kind of fungus in the form of a woolly growth often found on food.

N

nanotechnology
The study of how to make and use micromachines and other very tiny devices.

neon
A gas found in the air that glows when it has an electric current passed through it.

Nobel Prize
One of the prizes awarded every year to world scientists, writers and promoters of peace.

nut
A piece of metal, usually hexagonal, that fits on to a screw.

O

organism
An animal, plant or fungus.

P

parchment
An animal skin that has been cleaned in order to allow someone to write on it.

pendulum
A swinging mass hanging from a thread or bar, found in old-fashioned clocks to help keep regular time.

piston
A disc or cylinder that fits snugly inside another cylinder, but is still able to move up and down.

pivot
The point about which a lever turns.

plague
A deadly disease that spreads from one person to another.

plastic
A durable, synthetic material that is easily moulded or shaped.

plough
A large blade that cuts through soil and turns it over.

pneumatics
The use of air or other gases to move pistons and other devices.

power station
A group of buildings that house machines which convert energy from fuels such as coal into electric power.

pulley
A wheel over which a rope or chain can be slung to help move heavy objects.

pylon
A tall structure of metal struts designed to carry electric power lines high above the ground.

R

ramp
See inclined plane.

ratchet
A device that allows movement in one direction only.

reservoir
Place where resources such as water are stored, so that they are always available.

rotor
A device that rotates on its axis such as the rotor blade of a helicopter.

S

scaffold
A skeleton structure made out of poles put up to help in erecting or repairing a building.

screw
A spiral thread on a metal bar that can be used in a jack to help raise a load.

screw jack
A device that uses a screw to help raise a weight from below.

screwdriver
A device for turning screws.

second class lever
A lever, such as a wheelbarrow, in which the pivot is at the end of the bar.

services
Resources, such as water, electricity and telephone lines that are provided by companies.

sewage
Human and animal waste mixed with water.

silicon
A non-metal which as an oxide forms quartz.

simple machine
A device used to help in doing work.

spanner
A device which grips a nut. The spanner's handle works like a lever to help turn the nut.

spoke
A piece of metal that joins the rim of a wheel to the hub.

steel
A hard, long-lasting metal made by blowing pure oxygen into molten iron.

synthetic
An artificially substance, such as plastic.

T

telegraph
A device that receives messages sent as electrical impulses.

third class lever
A lever in which the effort is applied between the pivot and the load.

tooth
The part of a gear wheel that fits into a chain in a chain drive.

transistor
A miniature device which amplifies or switches electric signals.

treadmill
A wheel that can be turned by an animal or a person walking on the inner rim of the wheel.

turbine
A machine in which angled blades turn water or air to create power.

turning
A twisting or rotating motion.

type
The metal letter shapes used until the late 1970s to print books.

V

valve
A device that allows liquids or gases to flow in one direction only.

volt
A way of measuring the strength of an electric current.

W

web page
Information that is set up on a computer to be viewed by other people using their own computers.

wedge
An object, such as an axe head, which is thin at one end and wider at the other.

winch
A wheel on which rope is wound at the top of a framework, in order to lift heavy weights.

X

X-ray
A kind of electromagnetic wave that passes through the body and is picked up on specially prepared film.

INDEX

ACKNOWLEDGEMENTS

The publishers would like to thank the following children for modelling in this book: Nana Addae, Rees Arnott-Davis, Emma Beardmore, Daniel Bill, Maria Bloodworth, Anum Butt, Jessica Castaneda, Liliana Conceicia, Joe Davies, Ricky Edward Garrett, Sasha Haworth, Eleshia Henry, Sung-Kiet Hoang, Alex Lindblom-Smith, Sophie Lindblom-Smith, Laura Masters, Jessica Moxley, Aidan Mulcahy, Fiona Mulcahy, Seán Mulcahy, Joshua Parris, Jamie Rosso and Joe Westbrook.

PICTURE CREDITS   b=bottom, t=top, c= centre, l= left, r= right
Ancient Art and Architecture Ltd: 14tl, 44tr. Ancient Egypt Picture Library: 80tr, 80b. Barnaby's Picture Library: 20br. BBC Photographic Library: 41tl. Bridgeman Art Library: 18tl, 44bl, 50tl. Paul Brierley: 45tr. Bruce Coleman Ltd: 94bl, 94br, 95tl; /M Borchi 77tr; /G Clyde 87c; /Gryniewicz 116bl; /J Jurka 73c; /H Lange 67tr; /N McAllister 77cl; /HP Merton 117bl. Contour Colour Ltd: 8br. Corbis Images: 9br, 10tr, 10bl, 15r, 16tl, 25br, 29bl, 46br, 50bl, 54br, 55cr, 57tr, 58tr, 58cr, 59c, 58tr, 59br. Ecoscene: 94c, 109bl; /N Hawkes 81bl, 108bl; /W Lawler 82cl; /M Maidment 111tl; /Towse 112tr. E.T. Archive 10br, 14bl, 16bl, 18bl, 26tr, 27br, 31tl, 45tl, 48tl, 53tr, 54bl, 77tl, 86b, 106tr, 108tl, 113bl, 115t. Mary Evans Picture Library: 29bl, 34tr, 35tl, 91br, 94tr. G. D. A Ltd: 19cr. Hold Studios: /I Belcher 110bl; /A Burridge 84c, 113br; /N Cattlin 108br, 110br, 110tr, 111tr; /J Hall 82cl; /W Harinck 109tr; /P McCullagh 69bl; /P Peacock 116tl; /I Spence 87bl, 111c. Hoover European Appliance Group: 15c. Hulton Getty Picture Library: 38bl, 39t, 45b, 55c, 57t. ICCE: /M Boulton 67bl. Image Bank: 81tr. Mercedes-Benz: 55b. National Maritime Museum 49tr, 52bl, 53tl. Peter Newark's American Pictures: 54br. Oxford Scientific Picture Library: 11tl. Panasonic: 41br. Planet Earth Pictures: 67br, 81br. Powerstock: /Alex Bartel 95bl. Quadrant: 70br, 77br, 77c, 81tl, 86bl, 87br, 99tr, 101c, 103bc, 107br, 109c. Ann Ronan Picture Library: 9bl, 19t, 22tl, 22bl, 22br, 23tl, 26br, 27tl, 30tl, 37b. Science Photo Library: 21tr, 21bl, 21br, 23bl, 59tr, 59cl, 62tr, 62bl, 62br, 63tl, 63cr, 63br, 118cl, 121c; /M Bond 90c, 107t; /M Fielding 67t; /V Fleming 91br; /P Fletcher 98tr; /Food & Drug Administration 116b; /A Hart-Davis 87tr; /S Horrel 95br; /M Kage 118bl; /J King-Holmes 100tr; /S Ogden 119bl; /A Pasieka 92c; /Rosenfield Images Ltd 117br; /V Steger 116c, 118cr, 119cl; /US Department of Energy 120tr. Science Museum/Science & Society Picture Library: 8bl, 11tr, 12tr, 14br, 15l, 16br, 17tl, 17tr, 18br, 19cl, 20tl, 21tl, 23tr, 30bl, 31bl, 34bl, 34br, 35c, 35br, 36tl, 38tl, 38br, 39cr, 40tr, 40br, 48br, 49c, 49bl, 49br, 52tl, 54tr, 55tl, 56cl, 58bl, 58br, 76br, 91bl, 98bl, 99c, 105tl, 107c, 114br, 114bl. Spectrum Colour Library: 42tr. Tony Stone Images: 24tr, 46tr, 101tl; /Agri Press 74bl; /W Bilenduke 102c; /S Egan 67c; /B Lewis 111br; /P McArthur 105bl; /A Meshkinger 105c; /C Thatcher 105tl; /T Vine 88c. Superstock: 66tr, 67tl, 68br, 88tr, 95c, 109br. T. R. H. Pictures: 53b, 57bl, 57br. Zefa Pictures: 19b, 41bl, 101br.

Every effort has been made to trace the copyright holders of all images that appear in this book. Anness Publishing Ltd apologizes for any unintentional omissions and, if notified, would be happy to add an acknowledgement in future editions.